Pickleball Stories that Inspire

Co-authored by

Dotti Berry and Jody Belsher

Published in the USA
Blaine, WA
888-440-9780
connect@empowerpickleballwomen.com

Empower Pickleball Women

ISBN: 9798394135248

First Edition 2023
Paperback
Kindle

Cover Art
Dotti Berry, Harbinger Enterprises

Story-writing and Layout Design
by J. Belsher Creative
www.jbelsher.com

Acknowledgements

Mo Whalen and Carol Lo
for their expert assistance in final editing.
KarenAnn Broe
for her excellent proofreading.
All of the amazing women
who contributed their wonderful stories.

Project Support

Robynne Sapp
John Belsher
New Belgium Brewing
Civile Apparel

Dedication

We dedicate this book to all the
courageous women
who have found strength, determination
and connection in pickleball.

"Nothing happens in a vacuum without the help of talented people who surround us."

This project would not have been possible without the immense contribution of my co-author, Jody Belsher. It was my lucky day when I asked her to collaborate with me, and she said "yes!"

We each brought our unique skills to the table to make **EmPOWER** happen!

A Word From the Authors

We are so grateful to have been honored with so many amazing stories from such a diverse group of women. What is striking to us is the common theme of connection that weaves throughout the book. At a time of isolation and fear, many people were stuck alone while the pandemic raged on. However, pickleball managed to find its footing in this time of need.

Out from the ashes has grown a beautiful phoenix of light and happiness that radiates through a sport that is not only inclusive, but also accessible to all people regardless of age, gender, ability or otherwise.

Many thanks to all of the brave women who have entrusted us with sometimes very personal stories. Your inspiration will provide many others with encouragement, strength and possibly fuel to move ideas into fruition. Our common denominator, pickleball, has brought us here, to this book. We hope you enjoy reading these wonderful stories.

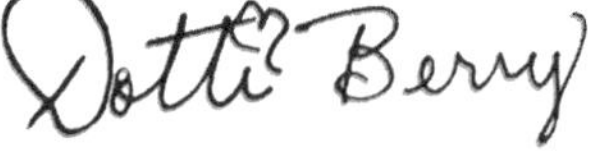

Jody Belsher

Table of Contents

Sarah Ansboury

Bringing People Together

My mom coached tennis and encouraged me to be a competitive player beginning at age four. After many years of playing, I had to have a spinal fusion due to the stress on my back. The injury forced me to take a break from tennis for five years. Eventually I got back into playing and started working at a tennis club as a pro. The club offered not only tennis, but a relatively new sport, pickleball.

I grew up in the northwest where pickleball originated. That is why the sport was growing more quickly in my area than in other parts of the U.S. In 2014, after being asked a number of times, I finally agreed to play in a tournament. I was encouraged by Mike Wolf, the President of the Vancouver Pickleball Club. I figured I had to be at the club for work anyway, so why not play. I didn't know how to keep score or anything else about the sport. I had no idea what was going on. I ran into an old high school friend at the tournament. I was impressed that she had just had a baby and was playing pickleball. That was the beginning of playing tournaments with Jill Braverman.

I won Nationals in 2015 in 5.0+ tennis and that same year medaled in pickleball 5.0 Nationals with Gigi LeMaster, against Simone Jardim and Corrine Carr in the finals. For a while I played both tennis and pickleball. That same year, on Thanksgiving weekend, a teenager ran a red light and t-boned me on my way home from the club. I was in my early 30's at the time. I had a bad concussion and a serious neck injury. I had to stop playing tennis because I couldn't serve the ball anymore. It was really hard to recover. I was in my room in the dark for days at a time. My biggest issue continues to be my neck. I also lost range of motion on my right side. Between the previous back surgery and now the accident injuries, I was facing some tough recovery time.

Most days of my life are about managing my chronic pain. My spine is compromised, particularly my ability to rotate. I also have stomach issues because the doctors went through my stomach during my spinal fusion. As a tennis player I had a solid two-handed backhand. But after the fusion, I could no longer turn my body enough to hit a two-hander. By 2016, I was playing pickleball full-time and had stopped playing tennis all together. However, I continued to coach college tennis for a short while. At that time there weren't many people teaching pickleball and it was not possible to make a living playing. The only way to survive financially was to offer clinics.

My wife Linh and I decided to get an RV, leave Portland, and hit the road teaching pickleball. She was a big help with my clinics. Pickleball was still fairly unknown throughout the states and very few facilities existed. My goal was to end up someplace to build a facility where people could come to learn and to play. The cards all fell into place when PPR (Pickleball Professional Registry) came to me in 2018 and offered to meet with me in Hilton Head. While there I met John Kerr, Director at Palmetto Dunes Racquet Club. I asked if he would be willing to put in more courts and he said he would if I would come run them. I jumped at the opportunity. By the end of 2018 we had 16 total courts. The following year we had eight more, making a total of 24. We are remodeling our original eight courts and most likely we will be adding eight more this year.

My job was to teach all the PPR people how to play. Today, in addition to working with PPR, I am also the Director of the Palmetto Dunes Club. What I love about Hilton Head is that it seems everyone is in such a good mood. It's a beautiful place to live and the people are great. I fell in love with this small town within two days.

One of the reasons I got involved with PPR was that I wanted to grow the sport and I knew the fastest way to get pickleball into more places was to get tennis organizations on board. The two sports are complementary—they work well together. The sport is now attracting a younger demographic and the game is growing in a different way. Since the tennis world has embraced pickleball the stigma of "going to the dark side" has mostly gone away.

With the increased popularity and awareness, more courts are popping up around the world. The sport is popular because it is easier to learn than tennis, with a faster learning curve and enjoyment factor, and brings people together in community. As the game changes a distinction is developing between rec and pro play, however, rec play will always provide an accessible game for all levels and ages. I love when I hear people say that it's their goal to retire and play every day.

I truly did not anticipate that our club would see families, kids and grandparents all playing together. There's something about it that people just love so much. We had a big group of 30 that got together and they were having a great time. We hold at least five bachelorette parties per year and as many bachelor round-robins. It's a personal sport. Being in close proximity when you play is one of the reasons it's so social. If I'm on a tennis court I can't have a conversation with my opponent, but in pickleball you are up close and personal. Pickleball creates a social experience that other racquet sports can't. It's so cool to see seven and eight-year-olds playing, admiring their talent and watching their drive to improve.

Another interesting thing about pickleball is that it's life-skill oriented. I have a friend with a non-profit that uses pickleball to teach underprivileged kids life-skills. I'm also encouraging tennis players to use pickleball as cross training for two reasons: 1) It teaches social skills —as it's more of a team sport, 2) It helps tennis players with the weakest part of the game: net play.

The sport has changed completely from when I started. Today I can make a living playing, but I mostly earn an income from my camps. I teach a little here and there but try not to be on the court teaching so much anymore. It's too hard to focus on my game unless I'm dedicating my time to training and playing. For a while my career as a player had to take a back seat. However, today, I have a terrific staff that supports me and I'm sponsored by Gamma, making it easier to focus on my playing again.

Over the past six months I have started working on building strength to develop a two-handed backhand in pickleball. I've increased my flexibility and mobility working with a trainer, a coach, drill partners and doing TRX workouts. Being active helps me keep my body as healthy as it can be. We work on core points developing mobility and creating more strength in my shoulder specific muscle groups. It's proving to make a huge difference in my play. I also do balance work, dynamic mobility and strengthening. I spend two to three hours on the court daily and vary between two-on-one, three-on-one and four-on-one sessions. My coach, Dana, is the best coach I've ever known. Although he is a tennis coach, he has a very good understanding of how to approach pickleball. He is tweaking my game a lot, making me hit harder and doing a variety of other skills six to seven days a week.

When I'm playing I know I can use my adrenaline to play through the pain. I remind myself that when I stop, I can treat the pain. Some days are worse than others. I practice mind over matter knowing that I will manage. I use massage, stretching, more stretching and a device to break up the lactic acid after I play. I know I need to be diligent about my routine to be at my best.

My plan is to keep going and see how long I can hang with the young kids, focus on continuing to grow my facility and my consulting company, and work to develop other facilities. I also want to help with training coaches to be the best they can be. With the numbers of people wanting to learn, there is a need for better coaches. The more easily accessible instruction is for people in this country, the better. I enjoy offering camps with Jill—we are creating some women intensive trainings.

A short while ago I was on the phone with a sports coordinator at a tennis club asking them to expand into pickleball. She said, "I think it's a fad that will go away." I'll never forget that conversation. Today they offer pickleball. I can say with certainty, pickleball is here to stay and so am I.

Ellen Awe 

A Cure for the Blues

My childhood nickname "Piglet" may have something to do with my negative body image. This always caused me to tread cautiously into most things that are either athletic or competitive. Until now, I've never developed any real skill at any sport. Since learning to play pickleball in that crazy wild ride of a year that was 2020, I can say that it's been one of the best experiences that's ever come my way.

When I sling my bag over my shoulder, pull on my spandex and step on the court, I never take it for granted. I'm here, I'm alive and I can play. It's the best feeling. My physical body sure isn't perfect, but it works. Sometimes it even hits one helluva drop shot. Pickleball was fun even when I didn't really have the slightest idea what I was doing. Fortunately, the first people I played with were nice people. They laughed with me, not at me, and encouraged me to keep playing. "Take some lessons," they wisely suggested and just keep playing. So I did.

In those early days, let's face it, I was awkwardly horrible. But dang it, I wanted to learn this game and I had more luck than sense. I showed up one day at a park and asked three men young enough to be my sons if I could play with them. I saw the wide eyed stares they passed between them before one of them said, "Well, okay, sure." The other two agreed and we played a weird game that was like the worst kind of first date. I thanked them and made up a place I should be so they would not feel obligated to play with me any longer. They were kind enough to bid me farewell and act as if it had been a pleasure. Wherever you are now, young men, I hope the world smiles on your good hearts.

Other times I played with people obviously better than me who were just rude about playing with me. Those times made me better too. I didn't give up and I didn't cry. Okay, maybe I cried—just a little. But I kept playing and the next time I stepped on the court with one of those guys I just did my best and determined they wouldn't have the last word of my pickleball progress. I didn't crumble and that was both empowering and surprising to me. At age 61 I keep telling myself that I'm old. But I'm actually not. I've beaten people younger and I've been beaten by those who are older. I'm active and I'm healthy and that's what's important. Equally important is laughing. A marriage therapist I once knew said that you couldn't have good sex without laughing. Well, I contend the same is true for pickleball. I can't have a partner who can't laugh. It just won't work. For me, it's all about clinking the paddles on a good shot and laughing our heads off at a bad shot. Pickleball, pickleball, how grateful I am that you came into my world. You are a celebration of life, a feast of friendship and a sure cure for the blues.

Melissa Ballenger

The Connections We Weave

My mother spoke fondly of a dear cousin in Nebraska. She and Mom had corresponded for many years. I was vicariously connected to my family through my mother. When she passed, I lost her and the connection to relatives I'd had all of my life. I did not realize this connection until it was gone.

Longing to know my relatives inspired me to go on Ancestry.com. I found two cousins close to my age and the daughters of my mother's dear first cousin, Embrey Ann. My cousins Jacquline and Clista graciously invited us to Em's 90th birthday and their family reunion in Nebraska over the 4th of July in 2018.

My cousins and their husbands met my husband and me in the lobby of our hotel to visit a bit before inviting us into their elderly mother's home. Once we met with their approval, we followed them to Em's house. When Em stepped out on the porch, I recognized her though we had never met. There, in resemblance, was my mother and a beautiful lady who I was so very grateful to meet in person.

We enjoyed three full days of events and too many relatives to count. On the final day, at a picnic at the local park, there was much talk and excitement about the last event of the day, pickleball. I'd never heard of it and I was too intimidated to participate, even though I had secretly longed to engage in some kind of sport for most of my life. The name pickleball stuck with me. I was determined to investigate it once I returned home to Washington.

The local club had a website but didn't respond to my inquiry. The YMCA informed me that they intended to include pickleball when the new facility was built. One year later, I took my first pickleball lesson at the Y. I was hooked. Not just because it was so much fun, but also because I was meeting the nicest people who I thoroughly enjoyed being around. Moreover, I was getting exercise and having fun doing so. This was not boring and I was, at last, engaging in a sport.

My husband and I began to notice that many of our wonderful new pickleball friends left in the winter for warmer climates where pickleball can be enjoyed outside in the winter months. We began to contemplate becoming snowbirds.

In early 2000, we took a trip to Arizona to find an active adult community that had woodworking for my husband, glass fusing for me, and pickleball for both of us. While there, I posted a few pics on Facebook. My cousin from Pennsylvania, who I had met at the family reunion and was the first to tell me about pickleball, saw the Facebook post and contacted me. Lo and behold, she and her husband were in Arizona, and they were only thirty minutes away. We met at the YMCA, played pickleball and then enjoyed a delicious meal at their beautiful vacation home.

In February 2000, a few weeks after returning, we booked another flight to Arizona and made arrangements with a realtor to show us what was on the market. However, in March, COVID hit. Our plans were canceled and hopes for our new snow birding adventures were dashed. This was hugely disappointing.

Washington State winters are long, cold, and wet. The YMCA closed temporarily due to COVID, and when they reopened time slots for pickleball were limited. We weren't able to play as much as we would have liked. Masking up to play at the Y during COVID was uncomfortable to say the least.

By June, we had come to realize it could be a long time before we would be able to start our new snow birding lifestyle. Instead, we made the decision to build our own indoor court and submitted an application for a building permit. With many unexpected twists and turns to the permitting challenge, it was 18 months before we were able to begin. Meanwhile, we purchased a portable net and artists' chalk and played daily at a local school parking lot during summer months, weekends, and after school hours when weather permitted. We met with others whose lives had been enhanced as ours had by this fun new activity.

It is now, February 2023. For the past four months, we and several hundred others have enjoyed playing at our completed indoor court, Big Rock Pickleball, named for the area in which we live. Often, we hear our guests proclaim, "we just love it here." Yesterday a dear friend, Bud, teased that he would like to pitch a tent in the pasture and just live here.

After fifteen years of involvement in the local art community as a fused glass artist, I decided to give up glass art for the love of pickleball. The transition from one life to the other began four years ago and has been magical. A few months before the completion of the court, I sold the equipment and supplies I had accumulated for glass art and took a course to become a certified pickleball coach. I have new students and returning students several times per week, and I absolutely love teaching. I am especially proud when my students beat me at the game.

Recently, the talented Dotti Berry, a co-author of this book, surprised me with a text and a picture of herself with my cousin from Pennsylvania. The very one who told me about pickleball to begin with, and who happened to be in Arizona several years ago at the same time my husband and I were. Dotti and Jacquline were both at the championship games and happened to sit near one another. And then they happened to start visiting, and realized they both know me. They were watching Riley Newman, who I had taken a clinic from last summer. The friendships made in pickleball are numerous.

Even as I sit here at my kitchen table writing this, I watch out the window and across the pasture as pickleball enthusiasts come and go from our court. This warms my heart and fills me with gratitude for the connections we have made and for the emerging of a new life thanks to pickleball.

Jody Belsher

Golden Years

In high school Mom and I used to play ping pong for who had to take out the awful cat litter to the alley. Mind you, the alley was dark, way in the back of our large yard and in the Chicago suburb of Skokie, it was typically a cold bitter winter. There were times we had snow tunnels throughout our yard. I did not want to go out there. I would do anything not to go out there. So, I got super good at ping pong. We played every night after dinner. We laughed, sometimes howled with laughter. I ended up on a ping pong team that won the state championship. I thought it was funny.

Sports were always a big deal in my family. We elegantly called ping pong "table tennis." My parents were both tennis players and Dad loved to go out and jog. I was very athletic, but organized girl's sports were not really a thing back then. It wasn't something I considered. I was a strong swimmer and was asked to join the high school team, but declined because I was rail thin and it was too cold.

My parents owned a music store and school. Mom played just about every instrument. I grew up with lots of music and eventually got a minor in music with a designation in voice at Western Michigan University. My dream was to live in California and write and perform music. As luck would have it, a friend and I each put 50¢ in and bought an instant lottery ticket—our first ever. We won $10 and thought heck, let's just reinvest the winnings. We bought 10 more tickets. The two aces and wild joker looked like something special. We looked closer and sure enough, we had won $10k. Nervous and elated, we drove home at approximately five miles per hour on the highway—afraid we'd crash and never see our winnings. When I showed the ticket to Mom, she screamed. Dad said that we needed to understand that some people don't make that much money all year. I always remembered him saying that and thinking how extraordinary it was. I invested my share and that summer it doubled and split. I had $10k in the bank and just graduated college.

I decided to make my way out west to Los Angeles. I was truly on my own. I had a new Camaro, my guitar, a suitcase of clothes and $500 cash with me. I didn't know anyone. All I knew was to go to UCLA and look on the roommate board and find a place to live. In time, I got gigs, recorded in studios and even opened a show one night at the Troubadour for singer Bonnie Raitt. I joined a band, sang at My Place in Santa Monica and wrote literally thousands of songs. It wasn't long before I realized I would make a lot more money on the other side of the business.

So I set out to work in the industry. After months of literally begging the HR woman, I finally got hired at Rogers and Cowan to do public relations for celebrities. I attended UCLA night school in PR and then USC Graduate School where I studied journalism. A few months into my job I was sent on the road with rocker Rod Stewart as his press agent on a world tour. We were in eleven countries, forty-four concerts and traveled in learjets and limos. It was quite the experience. I hung out with Elton John and numerous dignitaries. I had Rod's hairdresser cut my hair in a cool rocker kind of style. I traded my Beverly Hills wardrobe for English rock'n'roll wear. When I returned I opened my own agency and immediately signed performers, including Rod's band, comedians and actors. I had an office in a penthouse suite with a receptionist and conference room. I was still in my 20s, but was feeling very grown up. In my spare time, I rode my bike and started playing tennis.

One day I challenged one of my roommate's friends to play, having no idea he was a high level collegiate tennis player. He agreed to play as a favor to Susan. I told him I'd be in a pink tennis outfit. He dreaded the moment. We were both in less than great relationships and started hanging out after that somewhat awkward tennis date. We realized we wanted to be together and married soon after. Close to nine months later we had our first daughter, then 19 months later we had another daughter. We moved up the coast to San Luis Obispo, California, and had our third child there.That is when I became determined to be a competitive tennis player. I wanted to be able to play tournaments with John.

I attended the Bolleterri Academy and was soon playing at the USTA 4.5 level and attending regular clinics and getting coached at our home club. We had a great run. All three kids were high school tennis champions and we continued to compete. I played two years for Cuesta College starting when I was 39 years old and was nominated Athlete of the Year for being undefeated in singles and number one in doubles. However, my biggest feat was in the Maccabi Games (Israeli Olympics). Marching in the stadium in our USA uniforms with 500 USA athletes, was a highlight of my life. We both medaled in singles and mixed doubles. By our mid-forties the injuries were just too many. We decided it was a good time to close that chapter and I moved on. I took up sand volleyball, golf and racquetball, in addition to hiking, biking and swimming. I continued to coach six years of high school tennis as a certified USPTA tennis coach. I was also doing triathlons and half marathons at that time.

So when my friend Julie suggested John and I try this sport called pickleball, it was a swift “no.” We were not interested—period. She was persistent. She knew if she could get us out there, we’d be hooked like she was. We said no many times before we acquiesced. At first we played like it was tennis. Long, big, back swing strokes that sailed off the mini court. We were perplexed. We didn’t understand how it could be so hard to play on such a small court.

It took a solid year for us to understand the nuances and adjust our styles. Then, it was game on. We entered our first tournament. That was all it took. That was only two years ago. We have since won the National Amateur Championship and the Huntsman Games in our age divisions. We’ve won numerous regional and local tournaments and medaled in almost every tournament we’ve entered. We have our golden ticket to Nationals in Dallas this year and will compete at the World Senior Games.

Pickleball has given our 38 year marriage a huge fun factor boost and focus as we sail into our senior years. We are traveling, meeting tons of new friends, learning, getting exercise and feeling challenged. There is a lot to be said for having new meaning, new purpose and a new outlook.

My mother told me about pickleball years ago and I dismissed it as some goofy game. I'm so grateful she had a chance to see us play before we lost her. She competed in ping pong at the senior games and would have been thrilled to see us win in that setting. Of course, it was that refined game of table tennis that started all this in the first place. Mom and I spent many hours on the golf course together. It was our sacred place. We often would shred the scorecard at the end of the round and would wink that it was our secret.

A few years ago I went back and earned a Master's in Addiction Disorders. I've produced two documentaries on addiction and a third one that is an historical film. I started a non-profit (POSAFY: Prevention of Substance Abuse for Youth) to educate youth on the dangers of substance abuse. I currently have two public service announcements running on TV and was interviewed on NBC TV News Connection. I am published in several journals and have been featured on multiple radio shows and in numerous articles. Prior to the pandemic, I traveled the U.S. as a keynote speaker. I am passionate about educating our youth, particularly as they are now navigating such challenging times. I am also the proud Nana to six grandchildren.

Since starting to play pickleball, I created the Pickleball Workbook, a journal for the competitive player. I based it on the same principle that I used for the Tennis Workbook years ago. I've started several groups on the Central Coast for competitive players. While posting on Facebook, I fortuitously met Dotti Berry and we quickly forged a friendship and soon after, partnership for the EmPOWER book. I am grateful to Dotti for bringing me on as her partner. I have been inspired by editing the stories in this book. They have all touched me and given me great insight into the power of connection and relationship. At the end of the day, that is what everyone has said fuels them. Feeling like we belong, that we are seen, that we have someplace we can always go, is gold. It's pickleball gold. It's more than a gold medal or golden ticket to Nationals, it's even better, it's actually a golden ticket to life.

Dotti Berry

Rising Like a Phoenix

I first heard this unfamiliar term from Mimi Porter, who was the trainer for our basketball team when I coached women's basketball at Kentucky. Just hearing the word left me with more questions than answers. A few weeks later I was talking with a client and she said "BEMER has really helped my pickleball elbow." I said "What is pickleball?" The third time, I was at a conference in Scottsdale, Arizona and my friend Anne Adkins said "Let's go spend the weekend with my friends in Surprise, Arizona." I agreed.

We walked into the home of David and Aviva Goodwin. The first thing David said was "We're going to play pickleball tomorrow." Once again, I asked "What is pickleball?" He placed an iPad in front of me and encouraged me to watch a video. I told him that I didn't have a paddle and I had not brought any court shoes. He returned with a paddle and Aviva brought out a brand new pair of shoes in my size from the garage. No excuses. I was going to play pickleball.

We played the next morning, and I was immediately hooked. I returned home thinking "There's probably no pickleball in our tiny town of Birch Bay, Washington." Not only was there pickleball at the community center just five minutes from me, they had been playing there since 2014 and this was May, 2018. I got on Amazon and ordered my Z paddle like the one the Goodwins had loaned me. One Saturday morning, I left home, paddle in hand, trembling with nerves as I walked through the doors of the gym to where everyone was sitting. A lady named Jan Boykin greeted me with a big smile. My jitters left and I felt at home. Everyone looked like kindergarten kids, sitting on two benches, sliding down until it was their turn to play one on one on the two courts. Finally, it was my turn. I was so happy and filled with joy while I was on that court. I got to know a lady named Rhonda Saunders, and before long, we decided we would play in the Washington Senior's Tournament together that summer.

Two weeks later I was off to Hawaii for a couple of weeks. Of course I packed my paddle and immediately looked for pickleball courts. I found some beautiful ones along the water in Maui. I asked my wife, Robynne, if she would like to go with me to take a pickleball lesson. I found Pickleball Maui online, where Laurie Loney gave lessons on her back yard court. Roby promptly said no. She had been screamed at by coaches enough in high school; however, with some coaxing, she relented and we went along. Laurie and Pocket Loney were the best people Roby and I could have ever encountered for our first lesson. They were hospitable and approachable. Laurie's dad had started "Pukaball," as they call it in Maui, more than 50 years ago. Laurie invited us to join in on the community fun at one of the local gyms. Laurie and Pocket have been dear friends of ours ever since.

Flying home, I was still feeling stoked about pickleball. The man sitting next to me said "What did you do while you were in Maui?" I told him I played pickleball every day. He then shared that a family friend, Pro Tyson McGuffin from Chelan, Washington had just won a triple gold medal at a recent tournament. I said "Sir, I'm so new I don't even know of Tyson McGuffin." He laughed and told me I should look up Tyson online. Being curious, I did. I discovered Tyson was offering a camp in June. Having coached women's basketball at the University of Kentucky, I'm always interested in the strategy of sports, both the physical and the mental aspects. I was giddy as my fingers flew across the keyboard, excitedly signing up for the camp. Little did I know our hometown pickleball prodigy Matt Goebel, from Bellingham, Washington, was Tyson's doubles partner at the time. Tyson and I hit it off immediately. He offered to have me stay and watch Matt and him practice after camp each day. Of course, I took him up on that offer.

I felt like a kid again. I was tapping into something that filled my soul with a joy that I didn't even realize was missing in my life until I had it again. It's that connection with a tribe of people like I had when I coached in college. Playing golf and hanging out with buddies was always fun, but this was different.

Before long, I discovered there were Pickleball Ambassadors. We didn't have one in our area. I applied the following spring after I first started playing and was accepted. That summer of 2019, I was off to Tahoe for my first USAPA Ambassadors' Conference. I was going on you tube and watching videos, soaking in everything I could find. Just before I left for Tahoe, I received an email from CJ Johnson whose videos I had been watching, telling me about a clinic she was doing in Tahoe with Pro Laura Fenton Kovanda. I immediately signed up and my friendship with CJ grew from an online connection to a personal level. That is the magic of pickleball. It's the electricity that keeps my happy button going off all the time.

Before I knew it, I had attended my second Ambassadors' conference in Florida. I had barely unpacked my suitcase when the pandemic hit. I was in shock, much like the rest of the world. People were dying. We didn't know why. I felt scared and simultaneously confident that I would be ok. How couldn't fathom what was happening. Two sides of the same coin. Fear on one side and everything else on the other. Little did I understand at the time how this catastrophe would provide an "aha" silver lining moment for me via pickleball. Talk about rising from the ashes like a phoenix. Pickleball has provided that. I feel it saved both my mental and physical health. That initial engagement and connection that pickleball provided became even more important to me.

As we moved a month into the pandemic, it occurred to me that many people might lose access to playing the sport that fed them physically, emotionally, mentally, and spiritually, me included. I somehow grasped in the depths of my soul that pickleball was going to be our saving grace. Two sides of the coin showing up again. Many people in cold areas were being shut out of their favorite emotional space, the indoor pickleball courts.

With my background in coaching, I leaped into action and created the Pickleball MindShift Summit. The first person I got to commit was Morgan Evans and then senior pro Dayne Gingrich. Dayne and I had such a great connection as we shared back and forth about the mental game that I asked him to be my co-host. He agreed. Next I decided that I would reach out to astronaut Anne McClain , who had spent 204 days in isolation in space, to launch our summit (no pun intended). Was she a pickleball player? No? Some people questioned my decision.

They didn't after they heard her speak and initiate our summit. She literally blew people away. I felt like I had won a pickleball gold medal when I got NASA to approve my request to have her speak. I did have an ace in the hole. Anne's high school teacher, Shari Manikowski, was also a friend of mine. Shari was in the background encouraging Anne to say "yes" to my request through NASA.

I will never forget Anne saying, "*True Masters know there is always something more to learn.*"

Adapting and adjusting is the key in pickleball. My daily motto for years resides on a plague in my hallway. It says, "Ancora Imparo" (I am Still Learning), spoken by Michelangelo at the age of 87 after painting the Sistine Chapel. I felt compelled to focus on the mental game during the pandemic,. I knew that we were going to be mentally challenged in ways that we had never been before. I've used the word Mind*Shift* vs MindSet for more than 30 years. It's the minute shifts that we make moment by moment that truly separate and elevate our mental game and create champions on and off the court.

A situation happened during the pandemic that I allowed to take me out of my mental game, and yet it had nothing to do with pickleball on the court. My mental calm became a mental stressor. It was like being dumped by a doubles partner and not knowing why. My saboteurs in my mind were running rampant, lying to me and picking the scab of hurt over and over as it was healing. I gave them far too much power until I woke up, and once again tapped into my Sage, my authentic self. I remembered who I am, an EmPOWERED woman who is passionate about pickleball!

The good news is that the failure of that project turned out to be another silver lining of opportunity. Had I been entrenched in that pickleball project, I would have never created The Pickleball HealthShift Summit with CJ Johnson as my co-host, Pickleball Forum for Women and all the events we've done, Pickleball Happy Hour, ***EmPOWER: Pickleball Stories that Inspire*** with co-author Jody Belsher, or Pickleball Unites, my organization that collaborates to bring together people and resources for life changing experiences. One such project is the upcoming journey to introduce pickleball to Bhutan in 2023. I also am back to coaching the mental game in pickleball with Mind*Shift* Pickleball Coaching for Women with Coach Vee, Victoria Lopes. These events illustrate the beauty in finding the light from the perceived darkness.

I continue to be committed to a five step plan for improving my pickleball game: 1) Take risks. 2) Dare to make mistakes. 3) Get comfortable with looking foolish. 4) Honor learning over results, unattached to a specific outcome. 5) Rinse and repeat. Part of being an empowered woman is embracing these dynamic actions both on and off the court, harnessing my indomitable spirit. It about reversing the "em" in emPOWER to recognize that's ME, reminding ME to step into my POWER.

When it comes right down to what's most important to me, it's the people. Pickleball is just the vehicle for that engagement and unique connection to what really counts.

I've asked pickleball players over and over again this simple question, "If you had to give up one or the other, pickleball or the people you've met through pickleball, which would it be?" Each time the answer is the same, "I would give up pickleball." Ok, I realize it's a rhetorical question and we don't have to give up either. The point is that it's the people that matter. The tribes I've formed continue to be invaluable. During the pandemic we had a core group of ladies, our special little pod, who supported one another in every way. Friends Jayme Gilday and Jean Allen built at court at their home, just five minutes from where I live. We hunkered down during COVID. We called ourselves Shipyard Sisters after the name of their street. They are my soulmate sisters. Jayme, Jean, Jill Reimers, Melinda Henderson, Paula Tarleton, Karin Hoekema, Judy Nasmith, Felicity James and Megan Crouse. I don't know what I would have done without them during the pandemic. They continue to sustain me to this day.

And there's nothing like the comforting words of Robynne. As I walk out the door to go play, she says "Have fun!" and when I return, she asks "Did you have fun?" I refer to pickleball as the secret handshake that's better than speed dating. Pickleball people meet and within minutes, we're sharing our phone numbers and exchanging a quick text to make sure we're connected, forever.

Lynda Boesel

A Sense of Purpose

In 2017 my husband, Jim, and I were in our mid-sixties and easing into semi-retirement. We had both been self-employed and working from home for the past twenty years, and now we were finally able to cut back on our working hours. As a graphic designer I spent most of my time sitting at the computer, so I had always been conscientious about exercising. I joined gyms, swam laps, jogged and biked. I even participated in the 90-mile-long Hood to Coast Relay for a few years. But these days I was pretty much just taking long walks.

On the way home from one of my extended walks I decided to cut through a small park. Hathaway Park was only about four blocks from my house, but it wasn't particularly on the way to anything, so I hadn't been through there for quite a while. As I approached the park, I heard a strange sound, like an amplified ping-pong game. I was surprised to discover that the three decrepit old tennis courts that had been neglected for decades, had been transformed into six, freshly painted mini-courts, crawling with old folks in shorts and visors, batting a wiffleball back and forth with oversized ping-pong paddles.

All six courts were full, and there were a few players (I could tell by their outfits) sitting at a picnic table, apparently waiting their turn. As I walked by, one of them must have noticed my quizzical look and said, "It's pickleball, do you want to try it? I'll lend you a paddle." Noting the enthusiasm and apparent skill of the players, I was not in a hurry to make a fool of myself, so I said, "No thanks, I'll just watch for a while." By the time I continued on my way, my first pickleball friend had filled me in on the basics of the game and explained that anyone was welcome to play, you just had to place your paddle on the wooden rack hanging on the fence, and wait for your turn to rotate onto the courts.

This encounter rang a bell in my mind, and I recalled seeing a flyer at the gym advertising an, "Introduction to Pickleball Clinic." It didn't mean anything to me at the time, but now it did and I signed up that week. After three or four sessions I was ready to brave the unknown, and so, armed with a water bottle and my brand new pickleball paddle, I headed over to the park. To my surprise, one of the women waiting to play greeted me with a big smile and said, "So, you're back! Welcome!" That helped take the edge off, and when my turn to play came around, one of the men stepped up and volunteered to play with the newbie for a few games.

This was my introduction to Mike Wolfe, the godfather of the Hathaway Courts and a founding member of the Columbia River Pickleball Club. And in that moment, he also became my pickleball angel, taking me under his wing and helping me to be as comfortable as possible in this new environment. He played with me for a few games, helping me navigate the illogical math involved in serving and scoring, and introducing me to what would become his never-ending admonition, "Get up to the kitchen line!"

Everyone was friendly and welcoming to whatever degree their personalities or dispositions would allow. They were all shapes and sizes, and although most were senior citizens, there were also some thirties and forties in the mix. I played for a couple hours, rotating in and out a few times, which allowed for some getting-to-know-you conversations between games. I was hooked and I hurried home, anxious to tell my husband about my discovery.

Jim had heard of pickleball, and was pleased to hear that the park department had rejuvenated the old tennis courts, but he wasn't overly eager to jump on the bandwagon. In contrast to my workdays sitting at the computer, he had spent his working years laboring in his woodworking shop. Now that he was able to cut-back on his hours in the shop, he was looking forward to spending his leisure time in a more sedentary way, relaxing, reading, and writing his memoir. I was somewhat surprised and a little disappointed. During our forty-year relationship, Jim and I had often played sports together, slow-pitch softball for several years, recreational volleyball at times, and league bowling throughout our entire relationship. In any case, I was eager to jump in with both feet, and I was pretty sure that Jim would eventually come around if I kept on playing.

And did I ever keep on playing. With the courts being only a few blocks away it was easy for me to play every day, usually first thing in the morning, and sometimes also in the afternoon. Because I had cut back on my working hours, I was able to prioritize pickleball above just about everything else. I loved the game, it was so much fun, and there was so much to learn. Pickleball was changing my life, and all of a sudden, this semi-retirement thing was feeling pretty good.

After about a year of steady play, I felt I was ready to start entering tournaments. I attacked this new aspect of pickleball with the same gusto as I had open play. I entered tournaments within about a 60-mile radius, which took me to various courts around Portland and Salem, where I met scores of new players who shared my obsession with pickleball. Sometimes it made more sense to stay over Saturday night after playing women's doubles, because I often had an early start time for mixed-doubles on Sunday.

All my tournament play put a little more stress on my marriage, but Jim had seen how happy pickleball made me, and he continued to be 100% supportive. Although he never did get sucked into the sport like I thought he would, I always invited him to the get-togethers and happy hours that were by-products of my pickleball friendships. Through these social encounters, he has created his own friendships and bonds within the pickleball community, even coining the acronym NPS to identify with his fellow, Non-Playing Spouses.

In hindsight, I've realized that his not playing was a gift. The gift of having my own thing that I could do whenever I wanted, and the opportunity to establish new relationships with people based solely on myself, before they ever met my friendly, funny and charming husband. But in early 2020 it all came to a halt. COVID closed down public play. Thank goodness a Hathaway regular set-up a court in her driveway, and a small group of us continued to play through the summer. Finally, come fall, the park reopened the Hathaway Courts for public play.

Unsurprisingly, there was tremendous pent-up demand, and with indoor play still restricted, we had to make the most of it. It's no secret that here in the Columbia River Gorge it rains a lot in the fall, but in between showers we are frequently blessed with partly sunny skies. Since I lived close by, and because I wanted to play so badly, I took it upon myself to assemble the tools we needed to quickly clean-up and dry-off the courts: brooms, towels and blowers. And I also set up an online sign-up to facilitate connecting on the courts. Jim volunteered to build a broom closet so we could lock up all the tools there at the courts.

It was a revelation. We found that as long as it was at least 45° (especially if the sun was out) it was fine to play, so I'm sure the courts got more use that winter than ever before. Now, the online sign up, and the onsite clean up have become standard procedure. In the spring of 2021, our chapter president was stepping down and she approached me about taking over for her, since I was already pretty much doing the job. I was so flattered, and I accepted the challenge. After all, when the courts are only four blocks away, it's easy to think of them as your responsibility.

This sport has made the past six years the best time of my life. I've gained freedom, acceptance of who I am, leadership skills, and confidence. In addition, I have been empowered by the support of my fellow players. As president, I've learned how to deal with conflicts on the courts in a calm manner, and to keep the peace.

It is truly soul satisfaction when a member comes up to me and says, "You are doing a great job." It touches my heart. I love pickleball, and will play as long as I am able. Pickleball is not just a sport, it's a community, and it has given me a sense of purpose...something I have searched for my entire life.

Rachael Chatoor

Pickleball: It's Just a Name

I was a professional musician and my life was grinding and I loved it overall. The travel was brutal but the audiences were divine. Plane to plane, bus to bus, hotel to hotel—that was the grind. To be a part of top bands, as well as do solo gigs, was the dream of a lifetime for a musician. I had steady work, was treated like a rockstar, and was loved by an adoring audience.

Who would have thought I would be forced to give it up, and then choose to not go back. Nobody who knows me would have ever imagined that would happen. For me, it was an exit right off the rat wheel. My life as a musician was one that I loved. Had it not been for COVID and the pandemic, I would most likely still be living that life and may have never discovered pickleball.

Pickleball changed my life forever, offering me happiness and joy, plus time with family, that I didn't realize I was missing. I was walking my dog when I saw people playing and something connected, but I wasn't sure what. Pickleball sucked me in, like it's done for so many of us, and I am forever hooked. At first I thought it was a ridiculous game because of the name. And now, I'm a pickleball fanatic. It's given me a deeper connection with people that I would have never known.

When I was performing music, the crowds were intoxicating, they loved me and I loved them. But we knew one another for only a few moments during the show and again at the end when they stayed around to chatter.

Pickleball offers a deeper engagement and connection. It's a time of having fun on the courts and gathering afterward to share our lives. I discovered that I really love that. I didn't realize that something was missing until I entered my new world of pickleball.

There's an experience in my life that transcends being a musician and playing pickleball, but it's part of the reason I think I can do anything I decide to do. This life-altering situation happened when I was a young child and its impact has forever transformed how I approach life. For some, it might have been devastating. For me, it provided an impetus, saying to myself "Not on my watch. You're not stealing my life." I was sexually abused and my perpetrator couldn't face the consequences and committed suicide.

These are the facts. I can't change them. I realized that what I can do is to make a conscious decision about how I will live my life and what I will and will not accept. I will not accept anyone stealing my joy and happiness. This is why I am fiercely protective of my state of being through pickleball.

COVID is still around and yet life is returning to "normal." Opportunities to tour and travel with my bands became available to me again. First I said, "Find a sub for me." Then I finally said "Find a replacement for me." I'm retiring. What? Are you serious? Yes, I am.

With extra time on my hands, my creative juices had a new outlet. I previously designed apparel and other items that revolved around my music and guitars. Pickleball offered a new vehicle for designs. This blank canvas has opened up a whole new world to me. There's nothing like going to a court and seeing women wearing your ideas brought to fruition on pickleball apparel.

Together with Dotti Berry, creator of PFFW (Pickleball Forum for Women), we have collaborated to bring to life artsy pickleball designs that empower women. We discovered pickleballs in everyday life, such as butterflies, flowers, and peacocks. We created lines inspired by pros Lee Whitwell and Anna Bright. Similar to our skills in pickleball, these designs continue to evolve and so do we, along with the women in PFFW.

On my website I say, "We used to laugh at them all, playing a game with such a weird name. How judgmental were we?" This is likely why I wrote the children's book: ***Where Are the Pickles in Pickleball?*** My own reaction to the name triggered me to judge it, so I figured that if people read this book to young kids they will get excited about pickleball despite the name. Maybe when kids meet me in elementary school for pickleball month, the mystery of the name will be old news, they won't prejudge it and they might even look forward to hearing the pickleball story. That is my hope.

I like to think I'm bringing a different kind of music to the world in a new way through pickleball. It's like music being played on a court, where the people create a synergy that drives each one individually and as a team. My life was "until COVID." Now, after COVID I'm happier and more joyous than I've ever been, relishing each moment, one pickleball bounce at a time.

Lynn Cherry

The Pickleball Puzzle

I was extremely close to my mother. She was a mouse. No, not literally, of course. Even at a young age, she was shy and timid. Her mother held her back in school to help build her confidence so that one day she'd be prepared to leave the nest. While Mom's nature never did change, she hoped her children would not follow in those footsteps. She tried her best to raise the three of us to be independent and confident.

Fortunately, that early instillment of confidence helped enormously when at the tender age of three I was diagnosed with a congenital heart defect that required surgery. At the hospital Mom filled out the paperwork where one of the questions was "what does your child like to do?" Mom wrote that I like to do puzzles. This was clearly a sign that I had the drive to solve problems and an early indicator that I would persevere through failures—which have been abundant throughout my life.

Mom was a lonely, unhappy person living with my very difficult father. I traveled to Southern California from my home in Texas for a week each month to try to cheer her up. We were very connected. Unfortunately, in mid-December 2017, Mom was stricken with the flu. I went to help her in what I thought would be her recovery, however, she had decided she did not want to live. She requested I be there with her as she chose to starve herself to death. I can't imagine a worse thing a parent can request of their child, but I honored her wishes. I was there for her day and night until she passed that January.

My husband and I had previously considered moving to Connecticut to be closer to his family, however I did not want to be so far from Mom. Now that she was gone, we were ready to make the change. By April, 2018, we were living in our new home in Connecticut.

Knowing I needed something to do during the winter in my new hometown, I checked out the local recreation center schedule. That was the first time I had heard of pickleball. In my 25 years in Texas there was never a mention of the sport (of course, pickleball has now exploded in that state)! I checked out some YouTube videos and thought I could play even with a torn ACL in my knee I earned from playing basketball. I peeked into the gym, and someone immediately came up to me, put an extra paddle in my hand and got me on the court. From that first introduction, I was hooked. I went straight to Dicks Sporting Goods and purchased a paddle.

When I had open-heart surgery in the mid-1960s it was a procedure they had just started doing on young children. In fact, the physicians wanted to wait as long as possible before doing the surgery. However, it became increasingly necessary seeing a very active two-year-old jumping around and then plopping down on the floor, turning blue and needing oxygen. Understandably, I had a slow start getting into sports because my parents were concerned about my heart issue. They did not let me play competitively until I was in junior high school. Even so, I was always out front playing football with the neighborhood boys. In high school and my first year in college I played volleyball and basketball. Then I took up racquetball, playing at the open level in my area. I was almost good enough to compete with the professionals. My competitive sports background was a great primer that made pickleball a perfect fit for me. Pickleball also was a perfect outlet for me to process the loss of my dear mother and adapt to my new location.

I immediately became a pickleball enthusiast. Only a couple of weeks after starting to play, I put together the Pickleball Fire website. While I had many websites for small business ventures before, Pickleball Fire was my first content-based website. At the time, about four years ago, there was not a significant number of written pickleball articles on the internet. I thought I could add some value since I had graduate degrees in both physical education and sports psychology. I have to admit, I did not have a great plan for the website, but things started to come together during the pandemic.

With fall fast approaching I needed something else to do since indoor pickleball was shut down. I decided to start a podcast. At that time nobody else was doing a regular weekly podcast, and those that were podcasting were all men. I also had a background as a journalist in my teens and early 20s writing sports for local newspapers and health and fitness articles for national magazines. Since I was comfortable interviewing people and inherited my mother's relatively deep and smooth voice, I thought it could work out well. Typical for me, I had no real plan. As has been my usual mode of operation, I just decided to do something without worrying about the possibility of failure. Fortunately, this naive attitude has served me well.

When I started the podcast I did not know any pickleball players outside of my local group. I reached out to people with interesting stories and even some of the top professionals in the game. While some said no to being interviewed, many said yes. I did two shows per week for the first 150 episodes. On Mondays I interviewed professionals or instructors that typically included tips for players. On Thursdays I sought human interest stories about pickleball players. For the past year and a half I have produced two episodes per week. Currently, I still do a Monday show, but only put together a Thursday episode every few weeks due to time constraints. My time is much more limited now that I have added my new venture, publishing a magazine called Pickleball Fire.

I started the magazine just a few months after the podcast. I noticed there was so much content from the podcast that would otherwise go to waste. The core demographic of pickleball has been people 50 and over, and only a tiny percentage of this group listens to podcasts. That's when I decided to promote the written word—since us old folks are used to reading physical newspapers and magazines. The magazine comes out every other month and has been well received. It now goes out to more than 50,000 pickleball players. Unlike the podcast and website, I had to have a more detailed plan of the magazine, as publishing takes a lot of organization and effort.

I was recently interviewed by a writer from Sports Illustrated who was writing an article on the growing pains of pickleball. He was interested in how I was able to start a new magazine. I responded that I had been a journalist early in my career. He was surprised that I could make the transition from writer to publisher. As I had done with both the website and podcast, I was willing to jump right in without knowing where the journey would lead and whether it would be a success or failure.

Those early challenges I experienced in my life, coupled with the support I was able to get—and then give to my loving mother—gave me the inner strength to move into and through difficult situations. Whether tackling pickleball information or climbing other life hurdles, I continue to forge ahead, seeing them as puzzles to solve.

Darla Christensen

More than a Service Dog

My service dog Wyatt escaped our yard one afternoon. He ended up at our neighbor Steve Cole's house who just happened to be the top pickleball pro in Nevada. As I left his home with Wyatt he asked, "Do you play pickleball?" I tried to quickly exit the home of this crazy-talking person. I resisted his invitation for free lessons for several months, before finally deciding to visit his class in early 2021. I was immediately hooked and my healing began that day.

I was the security supervisor for the largest mass shooting in the history of the United States. This horrific event left me with a traumatic brain injury and severe PTSD. I went through some very dark times for more than two years, never leaving my house. My service dog Wyatt kept me from giving up. Just as I began to heal and thought I might finally begin to leave my house, the entire city was shut down for COVID. Another very dark year went by until that fortuitous day when Wyatt introduced me to pickleball.

My family started working for event security in Texas for the Houston Texans. We loved events and helping others. We transferred to Las Vegas in 2017 and felt so lucky that we had moved just in time to escape the devastating storm and flood that hit Houston just weeks after we left.

We had no idea that the move would put us in an even worse disaster. My two sons and I were working as event security for the Route 91 Harvest Festival Sunday night October 1, 2017, at the Las Vegas Village. When the shooting started, we could not tell where the shooter was positioned. It was dark, and we thought one or more attackers had entered the festival grounds on foot. My son Royce was closest to the shooter and endured almost 20 minutes of bullets falling all around him. Another supervisor pulled him behind one of Jason Aldine's tour buses, saving his life. Once the shooting stopped, he emerged to the main stage area which had been a highly targeted area of the shooter. He witnessed the fallen bodies lying all around the stage he had been protecting. Royce said it looked like a war zone. This area is where many lives were lost.

My son Ryan was in the main field area in front of the stage which was another highly targeted area of the attacker. Ryan witnessed people being hit by bullets and falling around him. He broke through a temporary wall, freeing hundreds and saving not only his life, but many more. Ryan continued to help and lead others to safety.

I was not scheduled to work that Sunday, but I volunteered to come in because we were short-staffed. I was the security supervisor in the main area and had the advantage of a radio in my ear. When the first single shots hit the event area we thought they were fireworks and were not alarmed. Within seconds a call came over the radio of a confirmed active shooter. I could hear people screaming and bullets hitting the concert area, so I hurried to the front gate and brought my employees and the event attendees back to the ticket entrance and out safely through a side exit.

I stayed in the main area directing the crowd away from the danger until we had a good flow going. I then ran to the street to stop the cars that, in their panic to escape, were threatening the lives of the thousands fleeing on foot. The police had all run to the area of the shooting or were triaging and assisting the many wounded, so I was the only person in my area able to rescue and help bring the wounded to the triage area. I knew my kids were stationed near the stage. I had no idea if they were safe.

Within minutes my son Ryan appeared in the fleeing crowd. We ran to each other and hugged in the chaos. I cannot express to you the feeling of relief knowing that he was safe and uninjured. The shooting rampage continued, and he helped me assist the injured and get the fleeing crowd to safety. Ryan urged me to leave with him and head to safety, but I could not leave until I found Royce. I continued to search for him as I helped rescue the wounded and terrified through the night and into the next morning. I received a text from my husband letting me know Royce was safe and that we had a miracle that everyone in my family had survived and was uninjured.

Eventually, the screams and sirens became silent. I searched the venue and found any survivors still hiding and brought them to our office about a block away. I had an emotional reunion with Ryan who was already there and we were joined by Royce a few minutes later. We hugged as a family and cried with relief. At 3 o'clock in the morning, we finally headed home.

As the morning light broke we understood the full impact on human life. More than 750 people had been injured, 450 people shot—many several times—and 58 people had lost their lives.

We have gone through the normal emotional swings of survivors and feel so much compassion for everyone who was affected by this horrible tragedy. We pray for all of the wounded and the families of those who lost their lives. One of our coworkers who was working near Royce was killed by the shooter. He was an amazing 21-year-old man who supported his large family. This was such an enormous loss. I am proud of my family and how their actions helped save and comfort people during the shooting.

Pickleball brought me back to life. I had never played any sports. I was a cheerleader and dancer. I started as a novice beginner in pickleball on March 15, 2021. I went to the courts and the players were not nice to me. I put my paddle up but the guy who was supposed to be my partner said he wouldn't play with me and stormed off the court saying he wouldn't play with a beginner. Two other guys tried to help me find a partner but not one person would go on the court with me. After a few minutes, humiliated, I left. I had heard how great everyone was but this was not what I experienced.

As a result, two days later I decided to start a beginners pickleball Facebook group to find players. We now have 4400 players in the group. Two weeks later I applied to be a pickleball ambassador, to help pave the way for women and to provide support for new players. Then I went on to get my instructor certifications. Years ago I worked doing office trainings for doctors and nurses and various other fields. So, teaching was natural for me.

I did all this so that I could teach players for free. My husband and I went to Texas to get my Level One PPR certification. That's when Steve Cole hired me to be a trainer at the Plaza to work with the beginners and help him out. I was a solid 3.0 player at that time. I continued to play and got my ITPA Certification as a level one instructor. I quickly realized there was a huge demand for beginning players to learn. I am now a double certified instructor, USA pickleball Ambassador and I continue to run the Facebook group. I put together tournaments at The Plaza monthly and competed for the championship in a Pickleball Reality TV show. I also work with other instructors to get them to commit to teaching one free class per week for beginners.

My game has continued to evolve. I train with Steve at the Plaza. Part of what I do there is marketing and each week I create and run leagues and a drop-in round-robin on Friday evenings. On Saturdays I instruct the beginner pickleball class, run a drop in round-robin and a skills & drills class. Once a month I run a tournament and a three-hour clinic.

My level rapidly rose from a 3.5 to a 4.0. My goal now is to go pro, 5.0 or higher, by the end of the year. I would like to play open, any age and senior pro. I train and drill four times per week and play seven days per week. I enter many tournaments and teach five times per week. I am all pickleball.

I cannot begin to imagine what would have happened to me if my dog had not escaped our yard that day. I don't know how I could have emerged from this life-changing horror. I am forever grateful that he escaped. Maybe that was divine intervention! As a result, pickleball has filled my life with hope, interest, community, reason and so much more.

Jo Anne Cohn

Living My Best Life Past 70

It all started innocently enough. It was March 2020 and I was in Ganta, Liberia. I was volunteering to help a small group of university agricultural students sell their homemade chocolates. My assignment was to help them write a marketing plan. The good news was that together we wrote a killer marketing plan which helped the group prosper. The bad news was that in March 2020, COVID raised its ugly head.

I was originally scheduled to fly through London to get back to my home in sunny Santa Rosa, CA. But airplanes flying through Europe weren't allowed entry back into the US. Many telephone calls, texts and emails later, I managed to get a flight through Ghana to Dulles and finally to San

Francisco. I thought that my ordeal would end when I arrived home in Santa Rosa. Little did I know that my world was about to change drastically. I was 69 years old—retired but with an active social life. Before COVID, I was an avid racquetball player, volunteer and social butterfly. My days were filled with helping others, staying healthy and being politically active.

I returned home to an empty house and an isolated world. Social distancing was the norm and I felt cut off from the rest of the world. Our racquetball club closed. Flying internationally to teach marketing to women's cooperatives was grounded. Visiting my family was deemed an unhealthy activity. I was one sad puppy until a friend called me up and said "Let's meet at the park and we'll play some pickleball outside." I'll be honest, I didn't even know what pickleball was, but hey, it seemed better than staying home and feeling sorry for myself.

That's when my life changed. I'm not sure Socrates was talking about pickleball when he said that the unexamined life is not worth living, but I can tell you that pickleball has clearly enhanced my life. When I think of joy, I think of pickleball. When I think of friendship, I think of pickleball. When I think of health, I think of pickleball. When I think of being engaged in life, I think of pickleball.

Pickleball has opened up a new world to me, both literally and figuratively. I've played at Nationals, I've gone to Turks and Caicos for a pickleball clinic and I moved to Arizona for the winter—just to play pickleball. And while it has consumed me, it still hasn't been enough. I've started creating pickleball content on every social media platform I can find. When I'm not playing you can find me uploading videos on TikTok, YouTube and Facebook. I now know what a selfie stick is and why videos need to be shot vertically. I even started a monthly column,

Dear Pickleball Warrior, which is like a Dear Abby column for pickleball players. I'll be honest, I have no idea how many people read it but that isn't what's important to me. It's just another way I can involve myself in the game.

And there's more. I'm designing pickleball clothes and learning about print on demand. I know what DPI stands for and why bigger is better when it comes to DPI. I'm using a designer from Sri Lanka and a manufacturer from Canada.

Because of pickleball, my life has expanded. My circle of friends is larger. My interests are greater. My skill set is fuller. And my zest for life has increased exponentially. I know that there are other women who are much, much better players than I will ever hope to be. I know that they are stronger, faster and much more skilled than I could ever dream of being. I know that there are other women who will be more successful writers and business people, and heaven knows what else better than I will be, but none of that matters.

Pickleball has enabled me to be engaged in life. At 71-years-old I'm walking around with a huge smile on my face. Because of pickleball each day I am grateful for the life I have. People see my smile and my joy and tell me I am their inspiration. I can only share with them that I am living my best life. It's funny, I used to say that I am old and don't have much time left so I have to make every day count.

What I've come to learn is that regardless of age, none of us have an infinite amount of time left. And I, for one, want to live my life to the fullest every day that I'm alive. That's what pickleball has taught me.

Kim Copeland

Feeling Younger All the Time

I don't really feel my age, except when I stand up after sitting for more than 10 minutes. When I was 60, I had my own business that mostly paid the bills, my daughter was in college, I had two dogs, a cat, a fish and small but wonderful circle of friends. I also had aspirations, many that hadn't changed in decades. Hopes, dreams, longings—these are good things, but I was becoming acutely aware that some of my most important hankerings had not morphed into achievements and that time is not an infinite resource. Then came COVID.

And then came pickleball. It started with four women who began playing on an overgrown, fenceless pickleball court just as the world began to tentatively ease pandemic lockdowns. I was the ninth player to join the group whose numbers quickly grew to more than 30. We were having a lot of fun and wanted more. There was talk of leagues, lessons and clinics. None of us knew about the wider pickleball world, we barely knew the game rules. It was wonderful to be outside and fabulous to meet new people. It felt so good to be active, like being given a glass of cold water when you didn't realize how parched you were. It was like taking a deep inhalation of clear mountain air when you didn't realize you had been holding your breath.

One of the women playing was my business partner, Susan. We had started a partnership the previous year and had been unsuccessfully searching for something fabulous to build a business around. One hot evening in July, amongst chatter and laughter on the court it became clear our endeavor needed to be pickleball.

We decided to create Lavender Pickleball Club (LPC). Lavender because of the color's unique historical significance in representing resistance, power and sapphic interest. Our group is mostly women and mostly lesbian. Through time, beginning with the poet Sappho somewhere around the sixth century BCE, the color has been used to draw together members of the lesbian community until more recently when it is also widely used for all who identify as LGBTQ+. As a group, our vibe drifted toward environmental acuity, being warm, inclusive, welcoming and having a lot of fun.

What could be more fun than hosting a pickleball tournament? It was late July and while it wasn't uncommon for snow in September, the fall weather was generally fantastic so we set our sights on October 2nd. The Lavender Pickleball Club First Ever Outrageously Fun Tournament lived up to its name thanks to sponsors, volunteers and to the more than 60 players who believed we could pull off a big (for us) tournament in a little less than six weeks. They came for the chef prepared lunch included in the registration, the fabulous swag bag with premium dry-fit shirt (13 colors in the artwork) and lots of other goodies.

At LPC, fun equals community. We started with four, and grew and grew until we are now almost 400 with a Facebook following of 1800. We expanded from Colorado to Arizona and now we are figuring out how to include Boston, Kansas City, Atlanta and even across the northern border into Canada. In 2022 we hosted 54 pickleball events from the everyday league to clinics with Irina Tereschenko and Helle Sparre. The LPC 2nd Outrageously Fun Tournament had more than double the participants of our first tournament. We have been in multiple magazines, newspapers and have been on television twice.

Until we started playing pickleball, I didn't realize to what depth fun could mean for our community. I didn't know that community could feel like a breath of mountain air or be as life-giving as a glass of water.

Now at 63, I have a pickleball company that is so much more than a business. I still have two dogs, a cat and a fish, but even more surprising, my wonderful circle of friends has expanded in beautiful unimaginable ways. The game with the ridiculous name has smashed my aspirations into action. I feel younger than I've been in decades. Time is a limited resource, I can't think of a better way to spend it than on a pickleball court.

Kelly Dakin

Remaining Positive with Pickleball

I've always been an athlete. I played basketball at the University of San Diego, competed in marathons, triathlons and completed five Ironmans. I was in a tennis league for 25 years. I first heard of pickleball in 2016 when they built a new tennis club in my hometown of Templeton, CA. Along with six tennis courts, there were four pickleball courts. What a waste of space I thought. Who would join a club to hit a whiffle ball around?

A year later I was protesting that the club was converting one of the tennis courts into four more pickleball courts. Who were these people? How could they even consider this a sport? Little did I know, in a few short weeks, pickleball would become my main focus and I would stop playing tennis all together. I was introduced to pickleball by my former tennis partner who had crossed over to the "dark side" six months earlier. I was immediately enamored by the unique rules regarding serving and the kitchen. I am a competitor at heart and was soon playing in local tournaments. The players were all so nice and encouraging.

Despite losing my first 3.0 tournament, I was hooked. When I found out they held tournaments all over the United States and even had a National tournament, I knew I had found my new passion. I didn't get to where I am overnight. I was very fortunate that within the first two months of starting pickleball, my tennis club hosted two incredible camps. The first one was hosted by Steve Dawson and Chris Mills. It was here that I learned the basic skills and solid foundations of my game. A few weeks later, Sara Ansboury held a clinic where I was lucky to get in when a player got hurt and I was a local on the waiting list. The pickleball gods were looking out for me! Sara taught me that pickleball was not tennis on a small court. A loose grip and patient dinking were vital fundamentals.

I was gaining confidence with my new skills, but I still had a big hurdle to overcome. I think most people coming into this sport experience this at some time, the challenge of breaking into established social play. I started at the bottom with drop-in play, enviously watching the better players on the more advanced courts. Soon I was invited to a weekly structured drills class. This was paramount to me breaking into better social play.

The ladies were friendly and the instructor was amazing. I laugh now because Kathi was my fierce competitor in tennis for more than 20 years! We continued social play after the drills and I met more and more players. It was here that I also learned that even though I thought I had the skills to play at a higher level, I had to pay my dues. I patiently played and let my skills do the talking. I was positive, complimentary and always asked for advice. I started playing in 3.5 tournaments and had some immediate success. I signed up for 4.0 right before COVID hit and never got to compete. Finally, when tournaments opened again, I played 4.0 and had great success, winning several golden tickets and eventually winning women's 4.0 50+ in Nationals.

Recently I have played 4.0/4.5/5.0 and had pretty good results. I also take weekly clinics from Dayne Gingrich in Santa Barbara. Having a good coach is paramount to excelling in my game. I have learned that skill isn't what wins tournaments. It definitely helps, but you need a partner with whom you gel and have chemistry. Tournament toughness comes from playing in lots of tournaments. In tournaments, you aren't playing the same people who you usually play against during rec play, so it forces you to learn all aspects of the game. I feel happiest when I'm traveling and playing in a tournament. I have met so many wonderful people, all different levels and from all walks of life.

As I was soon to find out, I was in one of the most wonderful communities of people and they were about to help me get through the toughest experience of my life. Pickleball brought me joy and gave me the opportunity to forget what I was dealing with in my life. My 21-year-old daughter, Annie, was a heroin addict. She was in and out of rehab, living on the streets, always a step away from death. Her addiction wreaked havoc on my 35-year marriage and my mental health. For three years, the pickleball community allowed me to escape my living hell.

On the court, I could forget about the drama and the stress of having an addicted child. My pickleball friends supported me through thick and thin. Then the day I had been dreading came. Two days after being released from six months of rehab, Annie had been found dead from an accidental fentanyl overdose.

My beautiful 24 year old daughter, whom I had hoped would recover and kick this insidious disease, had died. I was devastated. Never in my life did I think I'd be a parent of an addicted child, let alone have a child die. I didn't know what to do, so I went and played pickleball. And I felt better.

My friends in pickleball lifted me up and gave me strength. We held a celebration of life shortly afterward. We only told a few people to spread the word as I didn't want to post anything on social media. I was flabbergasted at the turnout by the pickleball community. Players from three hours away drove to show their support. Even players I didn't know that well showed up to support me. I felt so loved and so grateful for these beautiful people.

I never would have made it through this past year without my pickleball peeps! One of the interesting questions I am asked is, "How have you remained so positive and so strong through all of this?" It helps that I am a spiritualist and I find happiness in creating, crafting and art. A big part of realigning my life, however, is through pickleball and the wonderful people that find the same joy in playing that I do.

How Sweet it Is

The most amazing thing about pickleball I have discovered isn't the game itself, but the internal change and growth inside myself which was the catalyst for my relationship with my dad. It opened my eyes, revealing how much my soul was connected to the man I called Dad and the phrase he expressed to me: "How sweet it is."

I am on the court standing behind the serving line, my heart pounding, beads of sweat already forming on my brow. My brain is on overload as I find the best spot to place this plastic ball. I see my opponents are a right hander and a left hander and in my head I say "Perfect—go deep and down the middle!" Pop goes my ball! Gosh, I love that sound. I swear I can hear it as I lay in my bed at night, as I reflect on the games I played today. Contemplating, I ask myself, what can I do better, where should I have placed the ball, how do I slow that banger down, remember to turn and run to get the lob, and, man, my partner played great today.

The hours I have spent drilling, practicing my drops and playing are taking a toll on my body. I have tried anything and everything and taken advice on ways to improve my body fitness in order to allow me to keep playing. I have researched the proper shoes, the best warm-up stretches, and consumed smoothies that promise ultimate results and health. As I lay on my physical therapist's table as he pulls, tugs, and puts pressure on my body in areas, I wonder, "Is it worth putting my body through all this? Hardly a second passes and I say, "You betcha." If it makes me happy then I am convinced to endure a little discomfort. No pain, no gain, I remind myself. I am smiling as I close my eyes and drift off to sleep, dreaming tomorrow is another day, while I whisper to myself "One more game."

Pickleball fills my time up so easily. What did I do with my days before I wonder, but who cares. I have friends waiting to play another game, pickleball friends. Who knew I could meet so many wonderful people. Friendships that started with such a simple game. I feel so accepted, supported and loved when I am greeted so warmly with smiles and hugs! This must be how Norm felt greeted on the show "Cheers" as he walked into the bar each night.

I can't help but feel good when my opponent says "good shot" or a little friendly trash talk crosses over the net. I love saying sorry to my opponent when I hit a great shot, but secretly I am smiling inside and really only sorry I cannot do it again. My pickleball friends are like family to me. Pickleball has helped me build confidence in myself and given me permission to open up about my life to others. I have learned to put my trust in my partners on and off the court. It is an amazing feeling to have complete unequivocal trust in knowing she covers our sides, dropping shots, and setting up the perfect shot. Here we are working and thinking in sync; feeling that superpower and control knowing we got this! My adrenaline is surging, my mind focused on only one thing: win this point, win this game. I feel pumped as we accomplish what we walked on the court to do together as a team.

It is like falling in love and wanting to spend all your time and energy on that person. Pickleball is my new love. It is my addiction. I can never get enough, always wanting to do my best and loving this high feeling that lasts all day. I have a purpose, a goal and a dream. I want to tell everyone I know and meet about this game that changed my life for the better, and encourage them to give it a try.

I felt my inner child bubbling out of me when I first started playing. I would catch myself giggling and my mouth hurting from smiling so much when I am around my pickleball family. I discovered my mood was elevated to a joyful, stress-free, blissful feeling.

I was always a competitive person and sometimes my friends say I have my mean face on, but really it is my focus face. My sport has taught me there is a time and place for that, like in tournaments when it is all on the line. You know the anticipatory face when you are trying to be so patient waiting for the ball to become a little too high. When it comes I find myself pouncing on it like a lion after its prey. Patience, patience, patience. But I am not alone. I have a partner, teammate, and friend. We are working to bring out the best in one another, adding positive affirmations, and best of all tapping our paddles like it's a secret language between us. "Good job, atta girl, or that's okay we got the next point." That is what this sport brings out in me.

Sometimes I wonder who that girl is. But as I look in the mirror I remember I am my dad's little girl. I am a strong, smart, confident woman. Affirmations my dad instilled in me to believe in myself. He was a coach and athlete his whole life; It was not until age 54 that I discovered pickleball, the game that changed everything.

There are no age limitations or gender requirements. Whether you are tall, short, rotund, skinny; you and I can play anywhere in the world. Pickleball has taught me to be patient, trusting, supportive and how to let go and have fun while working hard, striving to achieve goals. It has especially taught me to be a kind, loving and supportive friend off and on the court. These were the things that made great conversations between my dad and myself. We found common ground in the sport of pickleball.

Having a lifetime of coaching and being an athlete himself allowed my dad to discuss strategies, help me work on goals on improving my game and develop a stronger mental game, which built confidence in me. I had it in me all along, but sharing it with someone I love while striving to make him proud of his little girl was such a gift to both of us.

Pickleball did that for our relationship. The day I won my first gold medal he was the first person I wanted to tell. I took a picture and sent it to him. He responded immediately with a picture of himself, arms draped with his medals and his silly grin on his face. “I am proud of my late bloomer and you have lots more time to catch up with me,” he said. Sadly, he passed away last spring. I sure do miss our talks, laughs and hugs. I truly am grateful for what pickleball brought to our relationship.

Now as I stand at the serving line I am no longer anxious because I know my dad is cheering me on from heaven and saying “How sweet it is!”

Tracie De Jager 

Do What You Love and the Money Will Come

Prior to pickleball I played many sports including lacrosse, basketball and soccer. Tennis was never one of them, however. I also did a lot of snowboarding and kite surfing. I was my dad's sports buddy. He had heard about pickleball more than thirteen years ago. He kept talking about the sport. In fact, he would rave about it, but I didn't give it a try for a long time.

It would be natural for me, as we had played a lot of ping pong growing up. It wasn't until we were on a camping trip at Thousand Trails Campground that I first stepped onto a pickleball court. They had a bunch of pickleball courts throughout the Northwest, California and Arizona. Dad showed me the courts at one of the campgrounds. They were having a tournament and needed a player to fill in. I quickly learned the game and played the tournament. Much to my surprise, I ended up winning the women's round-robin. It was a lot of fun. My first intro to pickleball and I immediately fell in love.

Dad and I continued to play rec together and eventually, about seven years ago, we entered our first tournament together. I was pregnant and playing. I actually went into labor playing pickleball. It progressed from there. I ran into my high school friend Sarah Ansboury. She asked me to play some tournaments. I didn't start playing seriously until about four years ago. My excitement for the game prompted me to go deeper. My kids were then five and three years old, which allowed me to put more time into the game. So much of the game is dependent on the amount of time you can devote to playing, learning and competing. I now have the kind of time to teach and play tournaments regularly.

I was married and working as a real estate agent. When I became a single mom in 2021 things changed dramatically for me and my kids. We were not in a healthy situation. The pickleball community rallied behind us and their support helped us to move forward. I now see what a blessing it was and continues to be. Those around me helped me to open my eyes and get into a better situation.

There is nothing like having the support of a community to hold you. The pickleball community was like an extended family for me and my children. I now am full-time in the world of pickleball. Where once it was my hobby, it is now my profession. That professional aspect has driven me to become a better player and in turn a better instructor. I want to be the best I can be for my kids, for myself and for the growth of the sport. It's an excellent choice for me to earn a living while raising my children.

Every day I am either practicing, drilling, teaching or competing. My parents are very proud and supportive and encourage me to follow my passion. My dad says "You only live once. So you have to be happy. Do what you love and the money will come." That is sage advice. It's interesting how the transition and growth of pickleball have been deeply entwined with the transition and growth in my personal life. The friendships I have made through pickleball have been incredible. Pickleball has been a major stress relief activity. Whether it's the camaraderie, the laughing or just hanging out with pickleball people. It also provides a focus—physical, mental and emotional.

The timing was just right for me. The stars aligned how they were supposed to with pickleball and life changes. I started out at a 4.0 level and then progressed to a 4.5/5.0. Over the last four years I made my way up to a solid 5.0 level. I was sponsored by Selkirk for two years and am now sponsored by Head. Selkirk sponsorship happened through a local scout in Oregon and then Head approached me seeing me play at tournaments. I was winning lower-level tournaments at 5.0. I started signing up for pro tournaments at the open division. In the beginning I was playing and traveling with Sarah Ansboury and some of the others who were playing, including Jenifer LeCore and Gigi LeMaster. I really did not have the freedom to travel as the others did. I had limited time as a single mom needing to be there for my kids.

I love competition. I have that athletic drive. I currently play at the pro open level. I'm an alternate for the MLP in Arizona. I play women's doubles and mixed doubles. I am ranked in the top 50. I currently teach at Recs in Oregon. They have nine indoor courts. I helped them open up the facility. My plan is to continue competing at the pro level for as long as possible. I enjoy growing the instructor side of pickleball. I am fortunate that my amazing parents live only ten minutes from me. Everyone who has kids wish they had my parents. They are an enormous help. My parents would come and make a vacation out of every tournament. My mom is retired. She takes care of them. I'm super close with both my parents. I have an older brother who lives in town. He has two kids. However, he doesn't play pickleball. He's one of those guys who just whacks the ball. I recently turned 40 and plan to keep playing as I age.

I am one of the fortunate non-former tennis players—one of 5% on the pro tour, who has been able to stay in the game at that level. Just being the athlete I am is what has helped me to become the pickleball player I am. I do a bit of cross-training. In the past I was doing other sports. Now I'm so busy with pickleball that I will go to the gym and work out, but mostly I spend my time on the court. I'm on the court for at least six hours per day. Every day I'm either at the gym, practicing, teaching or playing. On the weekends I'm at tournaments or out of state to teach. The thing I love about pickleball is seeing its growth and how it changes people's lives. All different walks of life can get on one court and compete with each other. It has shaped my life tremendously. It's really a special sport.

Leslie Eisenhart

A Mother's Love

In July of 2020 my wonderful 89-year-old mother was diagnosed with bladder cancer. My family and I were devastated with the prognosis. Mom had only six months to live. We cried, we suffered, and then we made a plan. My amazing daughter Natalie, who lives in Denver, immediately made reservations to visit every three weeks so she could spend time with her grandmother.

On Natalie's first visit, she mentioned that she had started playing pickleball a couple of months prior. Quite frankly I had never heard of it, but was elated that Natalie was so passionate. She figured if she loved it then I would as well. My mother encouraged me to take time away from her to 'enjoy life.' She was so unselfish! Natalie and I dropped into four different sets of courts so I could see for myself how the game was played and how inclusive everyone was. We hit the ball around a few times and explained that we were new to the sport.

People were very kind and started pairing us up with other beginners. I was a little taken aback because I had never seen such a welcoming community of people. I thought to myself, we probably just got lucky. The next day we went to a different set of courts. Natalie and I jumped right in and introduced ourselves and offered to help set up the nets. More and more people started showing up with big smiles, chairs, dogs, music and coolers. I said to Natalie, "All these people know each other, right? Are they celebrating something? No, probably not. Everyone just brings what you want to be comfortable for a few hours." I laughed to myself. No way. This has been happening all along without me? Next day, a new set of courts, and another wonderfully inclusive group of people. And again the next.

I knew it was going to be up to me to take the initiative to continue to play after Natalie returned to Colorado. And of course I did! Why wouldn't I? Everyone stopped and waved goodbye every time we left, welcoming us back and looking forward to playing with us again. I had not been able to breathe since I found out my mother was leaving me. The weekend playing pickleball with Natalie was exactly what I needed. Little did I know how this sport was going to transform my life. Not to overstate it but I actually felt reborn. I was exhilarated and a pretty good player for just starting out. Most of the players were in my age range and I immediately felt comfortable with my mishits and forgetfulness. Score, shmore. My gosh we laugh so much. And we didn't even know each other. This was addictive. My love for the game blossomed fast.

My brother, Russ, was on his way into town from Costa Rica in order to maximize our family time together. I was excited to share pickleball with him. Holy moly did he pick the game up quickly. We played every day. My mother could not have been happier that we were sharing this new passion together. In January of 2021 my mother passed. I was beyond sad but Natalie insisted on taking me to Mexico. I didn't want to go but I didn't want to let her down. I knew her heart was in the right place but I felt empty and depressed. She wouldn't let it go. I reluctantly flew to Cabo San Lucas. She was gentle but also insisted we move around a bit. One morning she took me up to the International School because she read somewhere on the internet there was a Pickleball group. Indeed there was. We played and I felt the tiniest bit of distraction. It was the first step. We played everyday with lovely people. One of them took us out on a dune buggy ride to a hidden oasis. What a beautifully memorable afternoon that was.

Six months later Natalie entered me into a 'Picklebrawl' tournament in Wyoming. Nervous doesn't begin to describe how I was feeling. I hadn't participated in any competitive sports since I had been in high school. The first night there was a round robin and I had to play 15 games with my stomach in my throat and very little confidence. After everything was said and done I took home the silver, or as I like to call it… My 'tarnished gold'. We tied for Gold by points, but after sorting through some numbers I placed second. Whew. Now I can breathe, or so I thought. The following day I played doubles with Natalie. She was gentle in her delivery of suggestions to improve my play. Honestly, my only goal was to make her proud. Until that week I had only played recreationally.

I kept muttering to myself to just get the ball over the net and to remember to breathe. I know breathing should come naturally, but I have a tendency to hold my breath when the ball is headed my way. Breathe. We pulled off a second place win. I was ecstatic and relieved that I could cross Pickleball tournament off my bucket list. I love to play, but I prefer recreational play.

In October 2022 I offered to play in a charity tournament when I was asked to partner with someone at the last minute because his partner had dropped out. Déjà vu. Nerves, dry mouth and low confidence. Darn it and again I was talking to myself- just get it over the net and breathe. I am very happy to announce that we won gold. Wow. Crazy. Over the course of the two and a half years that I've been playing, I have introduced dozens of people to the wonderful sport of Pickleball, including my two grandchildren. There are now three generations of pickleball players in my family.

I celebrated my 65th birthday recently with this whole new group of friends that I did not know before pickleball. We brunch and bike ride after we play on a regular basis. Natalie and I have traveled internationally on numerous occasions with the goal of acquainting people who have had little or no exposure to the game. The rewards are immeasurable. Natalie has also started a non-profit organization 'Peace in Pickleball' https://peaceinpickleball.org/ which is about spreading the awareness of the mental, physical, social and emotional health benefits of pickleball.

My life is full. My heart is full. My mother would be so very happy for me and I am the happiest mother.

Michelle Esquivel 

Into the Pickleball Light

My mom introduced me to tennis at six years old. I was not only good at the sport, I was dedicated. I went on to play in college at Concordia University in Irvine. My mom was my biggest fan and supporter. We were very close. My parents divorced when I was twelve and my mom raised me.

So when she suddenly and unexpectedly passed away ten years ago at age 60 from a heart attack, I was devastated. For the first time in my life, I felt like I had nowhere to turn. She had been my rock. It was instant and I was left shocked, blindsided. I never saw it coming. I lost all sense of direction—my purpose, my motivation. It felt like there wasn't any worth living anymore. I fell into a deep, dark depression.

To those around me, I continued to appear OK. However, I was anything but OK. Ian Liang, who is one of my colleagues and a coach from another school, turned my life around when he suggested I try this sport called pickleball. I am forever grateful to him. I'm not sure he realizes how much it has meant to me. I had become such an angry person that I relished the idea of hitting something hard to work through my frustration.

I transitioned quickly into pickleball and went all in to learn the game. Although professional pickleball was not my aspiration, in 2017 I decided to give it a try to see how I could grow. I was fortunate to be one of the first pickleball pioneers. In just a short time the game has exploded. I knew it would get to this. I had a lot of faith in the game. I quit my tennis career and devoted myself to pickleball. It was still in its infant years for competition at that time and it was easier than today to break into the winner's circles. I immersed myself into professional events. There was a lot of growth happening quickly but not a lot of people were coaching yet.

In a few short months, my life had completely changed through pickleball. Instead of wanting to give up on life, I was now focused and I wanted to succeed in this sport. I have since medaled in numerous tournaments, including the U.S. Open and Nationals. The positivity I gained transferred into my daily life. The journey has been absolutely wonderful. When I was working on my Master's in Physical Education, I was prompted to write a mission statement: "To bring joy and happiness in the form of physical activity with attention to inclusiveness and diversity." Most important to me is to make the game fun.

I started teaching with Engage Pickleball Camps and realized that teaching is a calling for me. There was so much I could do: play and bring happiness to others by teaching. Then I expanded and added Level Up Camps, which solidified my love for teaching more than actually playing as a professional. I truly love to see the transformation while teaching the game. It's very fulfilling to see people advance. I've gone on Pickleball Getaways, taught campers outside of the country and been able to see places all over the world. It's especially rewarding to go into other communities and see how they program and play.

In 2020 when the shutdown happened and everyone quarantined, I became restless not being able to travel and teach. That's when I co-created Ultimate Pickleball Academy. The idea was to go to communities that didn't have programming pickleball instruction. My partner, Rob Cassidy and I started traveling around the country. Word got around. We built a website and shared our info on social media. We got a lot of interest and so many calls that we never had to promote the concept. It took off.

Once things started opening up again, we scaled down our company and I became a Resident Pro and Director of Training Development at Naples Pickleball Center in Florida. I stayed there for a year. It was awesome. I guided the programming that included thirteen instructors. Seven hundred people came through every day during the season.When an opportunity arose to move to San Diego, I accepted the position as General Manager at The Hub—a new facility with 26 courts. I am proud of the accomplishment of opening that brand new facility, which brought in so many players throughout the community.

I'm looking forward to a new pickleball director job early this summer. I've done everything I wanted to do as a competitor. I always give my best and use my competitive nature to advance my game. I have partnered with some wonderful people and continue to play pro competition with the PPA (Professional Pickleball Association) and MLP (Major League Pickleball). Even though I am at the tail end of my pro career, I am still a strong player. I imagine I will probably want to compete again when I reach senior status. Today I am sponsored by Gearbox Pickleball. They have really believed in me and my brand. I'm grateful for all their support.

I wish my mom could see how far I've come in my career. I didn't know until I was 10 years old that I had been adopted as a baby. I always felt my purpose was to be her daughter. I always wanted to make her proud and happy. I have a good relationship with my dad, but since he remarried it was never the closeness I had with Mom. Her mother, my grandmother, and I grieved together—it was hard on both of us. She was a strong woman who lived to 93.

Last year I was awarded the female Fan Favorite from the APP by the pickleball community. I was so honored and touched by this award. If only people knew how hard it's been, what a rough start I had. My focus now is to give back what I have found in pickleball and the community. To me it's like a religion. Someone brought me to the court, introduced me to the others, I learned the lessons and kept coming back. It's a playground, a happy place, a place where you can feel like a kid again. To me it's a healthy habit that makes me feel good about life.

No one promised life would be easy, but this game has been a way to get relief from hard times. It's the sound of the ball. It's when the paddle and ball connect. You hear the sound and think of fun. It's so easy to pick up. The hardest thing to learn is the score. There's something for everyone—all levels, all abilities, all walks of life. Every day is an opportunity. The present: is a gift. I am so grateful and appreciative that my good friend Ian held the flashlight for me and I was able to see.

Jamie Elliott

When There's a Wheel, There's a Way

I had always been healthy and an athlete most of my life. I was featured in the Nov/Dec 2017 issue of **Pickleball Magazine**, with my life as a Screen Actors stuntwoman, flight attendant, and nearly 10 years of playing pickleball and tournaments.

At that time I had no idea how drastically my life would change. A month after the article appeared, I was diagnosed with a cancerous tumor on a rib, which I named "Earl" after the song, "Earls Gotta Go." A biopsy came back chondrosarcoma, a rare bone cancer. This news was truly strange to me. My husband and I were at our New Mexico home and decided to head to our home in Texas to get another opinion from UTSW. We were told that radiation and chemo would not work and that only taking the tumor, four ribs and getting all clear margins would be advisable.

So March 15, 2018 I had four ribs removed—no big deal—even though it was devastating to have my very first surgery at almost 68. After four months of physical therapy we gratefully headed to Albuquerque, New Mexico to compete in the Senior National Olympics. I took 4th place in singles and a silver medal in women's doubles. I was set to have MRIs and CT scans every 3 months. Unfortunately, only 12 months later another chondrosarcoma tumor appeared, this time on my spine. Surgery was set for March 18, 2019.

The surgery didn't go so well. The tumor, which I named "Jack" after the song, "Hit The Road Jack", was vascular, which meant they couldn't get all of it off and my legs were paralyzed. I spent 33 days of rehab in the hospital and endured six rounds of radiation to attempt a new procedure to kill the tumor. By this time I was in a wheelchair, and walking some with a walker with my husband behind me with a wheelchair. Almost another year later nodules appeared in my lungs. Once again, it was chondrosarcoma. I was put on an oral chemo drug and luckily there were no side effects. By November 2021, all but three of the lung nodules appeared to be shrinking, so I had five additional rounds of radiation to shrink the remaining three.

I was curious why I had been told that radiation and chemo wouldn't work. Maybe it didn't work back then but now it seemed to be working. Science is such a mystery. After 22 months off the courts I was concerned that depression would set in. I decided to buy a sports wheelchair, which I named Barney, after pickleball founder Barney McCallum. Wheelchair Barney and I have since played in five tournaments, medaling in three—one being The Hall Of Fame Tournament in Dripping Springs, Texas, and the other The US Open in Naples, Florida. I was the rookie out of everyone in the chairs. It's a whole new game sitting lower, your hands on the wheels and one hand with the paddle between hand and wheel. I try to play three times a week. I can also stand and hold onto the back of Barney and push. I have been doing PT three times a week for almost four years now. I do a water tank treadmill two of those three days, and one day of strengthening, and I have been driving for the past two years now. I work hard to get stronger, not sure if I will ever be stable enough to fully stand and play, so Barney and I just “pal” around.

I am proud that I am now a sponsored athlete of Paddletek and CNP (Chicken N Pickle). Drawing on my faith and strong family and friend relationships, including my husband, children, siblings and prayer warriors, I am deeply blessed. They have been there through my entire journey. Faced with such a daunting life turn of events, I have come to realize: when there’s a wheel, there’s a way! Keep the faith. Pickleball can help lift us all out of life’s difficulties and into the passion and drive to connect, work hard and have purpose.

Marina Fuchs

A Distraction From My Real World

I have always been a person who loves to play games. I was the mom who played sports with her two sons, the one who coached their little league games and enjoyed the camaraderie of sports.

We moved to Nashville because my husband at the time loved country music. I always wanted to do the things that would make him happy. However, my marriage was a series of me doing something wrong. For 35 years I apologized. During the last fight I simply didn't apologize anymore. He didn't talk to me for six months. I was lost.

We first learned about pickleball in Nashville, Tennessee on vacation in June of 2021. We bought a starter set and played on a tennis court in our development. It didn't work out very well and the paddles got stored at home. I googled pickleball in my area. There were courts only five miles from my apartment. I took my beginner paddle to the court. The first person I met told me I have a toy paddle. I was so nervous going there on my own, but I couldn't just wallow in self-pity all day. I needed an escape. I had played paddle ball as a kid and I had taken one month of tennis lessons. I loved that, so I figured I might be pretty good at pickleball.

My son, who is my rock, took me to the store to buy my first real paddle. I started to go often to play and I immediately fell in love with the sport. I hadn't done much physical activity in a long time and it felt great. My cousin also started to play, and together we explored some beautiful courts. The people were all so welcoming. Some participants were just starting this journey and others I could see already had the bug. I did this for a couple of months and I was able to be distracted from the life I tried so hard to perfect. I wanted to be the perfect wife, always trying to hold down the fort but always having a pit in my stomach. On the court all that went away. Life continued to get more complicated. I found I needed to run away from it all.

I went to a relative's house who took me in with open arms. The first thing I did was search on a local Facebook page where I could find a pickleball court. I found a nearby park. The first woman I met turned out to be a good friend. She also found this game at a crucial time in her life. She has found empowerment with the game. She took my number and we began to talk about pickleball: what time are we meeting, where are the places in the area that we can play, etc.

The networking starts to fill my days of loneliness. One day, when I broke my paddle during a game, I started to cry. I didn't want anything to keep me from playing. My son thoughtfully mailed me a new paddle and had it engraved "forever your anchor." It is a lyric from a song that he wrote. I was elated and touched. I decided to play in a tournament. I didn't have a partner so they assigned me one. Incredibly, we won gold together. I was so thrilled that I sent a photo to my kids and friends. They were all very proud of me. I find I am very excited for the first time in a long while.

After 30 years of marriage, I filed for divorce. This caused me to leave my second place of residence. I booked a flight, but I had promised my first pickleball friend I wouldn't leave until I played a tournament with her. I brought my suitcase to the tournament and stuck it in her car. We didn't win, but she was grateful we got to play together. I headed out to my third place of residence within a year. A friend had already scouted out a park that has pickleball. I remember the feeling of walking from the parking lot trying to find the court. I could hear the sound of the paddle hitting the ball; it's a sound that brings me joy. I met some wonderful people and joined the community. I'm even going to get my rating in a few weeks.

One of the women I met said: " I love to play with you." I've heard this kind remark from a number of people. I believe when you enjoy something as much as I do and meet people with the same passion, it brings us all together. Pickleball has given me a new outlook on life. It is my distraction from the real world.

Lisa Galey

More Than Just Pickleball

I am a fierce and loving momma of three kids. I feel deep joy in our connection and deep hurt in our pain. When my son was 12 years old and at a boarding school in Albuquerque, I was feeling a mother's emptiness in his absence. I was also struggling with many personal life challenges. The difficulties seemed to keep me from living for myself. It had been a long time since I had thought about doing something for myself.

I was introduced to a new sport in January 2022. Pickleball was the catalyst to a beautiful emergence of self. It was as if I had been sleeping and suddenly long dormant parts of me awoke. It re-ignited my athletic passion and my practice of diving deep. I was excited and eager to learn. I began spending a lot of time on the court, learning about drop-in etiquette, watching the pros play on YouTube and Facebook, talking to others about the game and buying equipment. I watched so much pickleball that my kids would roll their eyes and say with judgment, "You're watching pickleball again." The answer was of course, yes.

I took my first lesson with a group called Lavender Pickleball Club in Colorado. The game has been an integral part of my life ever since. At that lesson about a year and a half ago I knew I was going to dive deep into learning the technical and strategic aspects of the game and put the hours in to improve. I had to work through layers of vulnerability and physical setbacks. Those were new hard lessons for me.

Being part of something special is important for our health. Many of us have some trepidation when stepping into something new. I am very private. I had to soften, which took some introspection. It took me a while to make changes. Some people are challenged by the technical part of the game. Some find the social-emotional aspect uncomfortable. Once someone gets past the hesitancy they typically experience the enjoyment of the game and the friendships that form from drop-in groups, lessons or just chatting with someone who lights up when you say the word pickleball.

I now have a lifetime friend that I didn't even know a year ago. We were both newbies and it was a lovely connection because I didn't feel alone in my journey. I made friends with people that at first I was resistant to get to know. Making new friends wasn't what I was seeking at 55 years old, however, I found a new tribe which has been tremendously enriching for me. I now grow friendships along with growing myself. I realize now the silver lining of the challenges I struggled with prior to pickleball. Those issues prompted me to seek out pickleball, which has opened a new world for me. My son is home now and gets to see my passion for being a momma but also for playing a game I love. What a beautiful duality.

Physically I am strong but because I played so often and didn't give my body a chance to catch up I was on crutches twice. The big lessons about patience were so hard. I expected way more of my body than it could support and I felt sad and mad that I perceived my body as being "broken." There was a huge relearning for me that my body is my life vessel. My only choice was to slow down and repair. During those injuries I continued to play with my pickleball partner. She never asked me to be or do more than I could. She lifted me up and met me where I was. We would just dink so I didn't have to run around and that was good enough.

Sometimes I felt like a bird getting let out of a cage—a great sense of freedom. I learned that community and doubles partners were just as important as winning. In that growth I learned how to support (my partners and myself). Early on I had nicknames that were indicative of how people perceived me which included "bullet" and "rocket." I am happy and grateful that some of those same people are now my friends and see me as a competitive person, as well as a supportive and passionate one that loves life and pickleball.

I can now embrace, and even say, that I am a good pickleball player. It took some time and work on a very personal level for me to say that out loud. In the same breath I can say that sharing the experience with others is just as important. I lift them up and they lift me. We've all experienced the good days as well as those bad ones. The game of pickleball has changed me in many ways, so much so that I would love to coach one day. I already have my pickleball training schedule figured out. Pickleball is more than getting exercise, having fun and building community. It's an amazing and awesome journey and so much more. I love life. I love pickleball.

Kasandra Gehrke 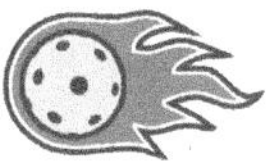

How Hasn't Pickleball Changed My Life?

As a child I played volleyball, softball and basketball. I loved playing sports. I grew up in Wisconsin where I attended high school and college. As a young university student, I studied physical education and went directly into teaching middle and high school P.E. During my three years as a teacher, I was always looking for something fun and exciting for the students to do.

There just weren't many group sports that were attractive at the time. Then one day, while working out at the gym, I noticed people playing an unusual sport. I watched for a while, wondering how it was played. Suddenly, they needed a fourth. I jumped right in, figuring the three 70 year old plus athletes would be no contest for me. Clearly, I was mistaken. They beat me every game. I could not believe they were whooping me. Even so, I was taken with the sport. Soon it would dominate my life.

Immediately after I got home, I went on eBay and ordered a paddle—choosing one in a color I thought was nice, not caring about the brand or quality. I began playing at the gym. It wasn't long before I signed up for one of their small local tournaments. To my surprise, I won the tournament. That was the impetus that charged me to seek out other tournaments. The feeling of competing again, like I did in high school sports, was thrilling for me. I didn't realize how much I enjoyed that feeling and how much I had been missing competitive sports.

That was seven years ago. I was 27 years old and from the start most definitely addicted to pickleball. Fortunately, I was able to learn from Dave Weinbach, a top pro who lived in Wisconsin. There weren't many good players on the scene yet in 2016. He and I played a tournament together. I helped Dave teach clinics—which were new for the sport. However, I found my time was limited since I was still teaching and could only participate in pickleball after work hours and on weekends.

I wasn't making much money as a teacher, so I thought why not give it a try as a pickleball pro and coach. I called my mom and she helped me decide to dedicate a year to make a run as a pro player and see what happened. My goal was literally to be able to survive financially. It was a rather quick transition from beginner to pro. My first tournament was at 3.5, then I spent a summer as a 4.0 and won all the tournaments I entered. Soon I was at 4.5 and then boom, 5.0.

I didn't play any college sports and subsequently gained a lot of weight. After finding pickleball, I began living a more healthy lifestyle. I lost about 60 pounds.

My newfound sport and career brought back the joy and happiness that was missing. I met so many new people. I feel like I now have family all over the country. I can call someone in most states as host homes—they are like an extended family to me. If I go back to Kentucky, there's a family there that welcomes me. It's so unbelievable. The connections, the people. I love everything about what I do. I took a chance on pickleball and it turns out I made the right decision. It has worked out better than I ever imagined. I love to travel, stay in hotels, see new places, and meet new people. When asked how pickleball changed my life, I say, how hasn't it changed my life!

I realize that my time as a pro is limited. As the game amps up to a higher caliber of players, former tennis stars and younger ages, it is important for me to consider my future. My love of teaching is a perfect blend of my skill set and athleticism. As a result, I've created my women-focused company, EmpowHer, and started offering camps, clinics and trips exclusively for women. Providing a space for women gives them a comfort level and different vibe. It is proving to be successful, as my first trip filled up immediately with 80 players.

Previously, a pro could get by practicing a few times a week. Now it has become a full-time job for many. In the beginning you didn't see support around a pro. Now they have coaches, therapists, managers, sponsors, etc. To be a pro today you have to devote yourself to the game. It's hard mentally and physically to teach—giving a lot of yourself on the court—with not enough energy left to train. Before you could get away with that, but not anymore. Where it was once ok to compete on the side, now it is necessary to devote eight hours a day to be a pro—as it should be. I plan to continue playing at least another year as a pro and focus on branding my company and developing the teaching side of pickleball. As pickleball grows up into a mature sport, we are now seeing it offered on the collegiate level, young kids playing in school, leagues of all ages and a full tournament schedule.

In spring 2020, fellow pro Lee Whitwell and I were hosted by a family for the St. Louis Open. We typically play with our hosts as a thank you. That weekend the hosts invited two guys to come hit with us. One was a guy named Caleb Fall. He was about a 3.5 player. Something about him stuck with me. We didn't exchange numbers, however, Ironically, a friend told me about a guy she played against in a tournament named Caleb. I said, "Does he have a big beard?" She said "Yes." I asked her to get his contact info. I wanted to get to know him. The minute he got my cell number he texted me and we went on our first date. We have been together ever since. In fact, he has worked very hard on his game and is now competing along with me at the 5.0 level. We are scheduled to play together as a mixed doubles team at the U.S. Open.

I am truly enjoying my life, especially having Caleb and my trusty golden retriever Finley by my side. Finley lovingly greets everybody. My best event so far was winning a bronze medal with Zane Navratil at the 2019 U.S. Open. It was such an exciting win. At the time there were only three majors: Nationals, U.S. Open and the Tournament of Champions. So it was a big deal to win a medal. It was amazing being on the big stage—the whole stadium watching and cheering. It was electric, a memory I will always cherish.

The lifestyle I have chosen requires a lot of travel, change and commitment. I think of my life as controlled chaos. I'd be bored without pickleball and all that it involves. I also think it's good to find balance and to give it your best, while at the same time having a realistic view of the big picture and the future. I feel very grateful for my life today

Brandi Givens

A Special Sense of Inclusion

My husband and I had just taken a spin class together, hoping that long-distance biking would be a healthy hobby that we could enjoy together. As we were exiting the YMCA in Starwood, Washington that morning in March 2018, tired and saddle-sore, we passed the basketball gymnasium. There, a boisterous group of people was playing a funny little game with paddles and a yellow whiffleball. Intrigued by all the laughter and banter, we stopped to watch in the doorway. After noticing our gawking for a few minutes, an athletic-looking woman who had been dominating the game insisted we come into the gym and try this sport she called "pickleball." Without hesitation we obeyed, my husband confiding to me in a whisper, "I'm going to dominate."

We never took another spin class.

I'm a registered dietitian, mother of two adult children, and wife to a fellow pickleball addict. My obsession with this wonderful sport started during a transitional point in my life. My husband had recently retired from the Navy after 24 years of service, our kids had all too quickly become young adults, and I had just lost my adored father to cancer. So, while trying to heal from my terrible loss, I was also finding my place in the civilian world without kiddos who needed me daily. I was overwhelmed with sadness, and lonely without my military community.

In those first days of learning the basics of the game, I was surrounded by some of the most welcoming people I'd ever met. They patiently encouraged my progress. This was an important component for me since I'm not a naturally confident person and may never have picked up a paddle again if the other players had been less friendly. Seeing that we were serious about learning, high-level players quickly took us under their wings to help us improve. They wanted nothing in return, some only suggesting that we pay it forward.

This special sense of inclusion seems to be a common theme in pickleball as I've heard similar stories time and again. I personally believe that the friendly nature of most players can be easily explained. When people are playing pickleball, it makes them happy, and they want to share that joy with others. It's that simple. Regardless of why the players were kind to me, I was greeted with open arms at a time when I needed it most. Some of the connections that sprouted during those laughter-filled moments have grown into deep friendships that I didn't know could exist outside of our military family.

As with many people, it wasn't long before playing became a must. We began competing in tournaments, near and far. As a commercial pilot, work was not a tournament obstacle for my husband, as he could create his own schedule. I, on the other hand, had two jobs: one as a dietitian in an office, and the other as an escape room business owner.

I decided to quit my desk job and try using my nutrition expertise as a writer, so that my hours spent working were more flexible. My first writing break was published in Pickleball Magazine with an article called "Snack Like a Pro" in which I got to interview several professional pickleball players. I've written for the magazine ever since, and now have a column called "In the Kitchen with Brandi." I credit Pickleball Magazine for my start, and I currently write health and nutrition content for multiple websites.

By early 2020, my husband and I realized that the daily Washington drizzle kept us off the courts way too often. When COVID shut our escape room down, we decided it was time to take advantage of our flexible jobs and become early snowbirds. By mid-2020 we found a winter place in Surprise, Arizona so that we could play ball all year. Surprise has a beautiful community park with 16 dedicated pickleball courts. It's known as a mecca where a wide range of levels can find a place to play.

Wintering in Surprise probably would have been enough for most people, but somehow, we weren't satisfied. What we really wanted was to build our own courts and have a living space big enough to share them with family and the great friends we'd met along the way.

In 2022 we found just the right home in Surprise with an acre of land and, most importantly, no homeowners association to keep us from building our courts, which we did. I hear the cheering and joking of my husband and seven other gentlemen just outside my window, along with the pop,

pop, pop of that wonderful yellow ball. It's music to my ears as I anticipate my own group of friends arriving in a few hours.

Pickleball means so much that my entire lifestyle has changed. It means sidestepping into a fun new career, and moving to a place I never knew I wanted to live. It means knowing I might find meaningful friendships during my next casual rec day on the courts. It means spending our savings to build courts in our backyard for a sport we didn't even know existed five years ago. It means healing from great loss. It means we redefined our sense of community. It means the potential for happiness every single day.

Yvonne Hackenberg 

A Long Life in Sport

I am a wife, mother (to Kristy) and grandmother (Tyler, Riley and JR). I have had a lifelong love of sports that is shared by my family. My sports background includes tennis, platform tennis and paddleball. My participation in platform tennis and paddle ball resulted in multiple national titles and induction into the Platform Tennis Hall of Fame. Thank you to my doubles partners Jim Hackenberg, Hilary Marold, Robin Fulton, Linda Wolf and Caprice Behner.

Then pickleball came along. On a fateful day in 2009 my husband, Jim, and I saw an article in our local newspaper regarding pickleball being offered at our local YMCA. We had already heard murmurings about pickleball from Jim's uncle, who lived in The Villages. We decided to head to the Y and check it out. Our local ambassadors, Melissa Muha and

Bob Northrup, were very welcoming. Equipment was provided and after the first ball was struck we never looked back.

Our background in platform tennis made the transition moderately easy. The court is the same size, and the net height is the same. After playing for a couple of months, we decided to test the waters and headed to Arizona to play in the Nationals in Buckeye. I had a lock on Jim for mixed, but I needed a women's partner. I knew that my longtime doubles partner in platform tennis, Hilary Marold, would be a natural at my new sport. She agreed and a partnership was rekindled that led to multiple pickleball titles, including Nationals, the US Open and The Tournament of Champions. I am proud to say that the vast majority of my titles came with Jim and Hilary by my side. It was a proud and grateful moment when Jim, Hilary and I were inducted into the Pickleball Hall of Fame in 2020 and 2021, respectfully.

The most remarkable part of my story is the fact that four generations of my family are active in the sport. The person who gets the most recognition when we arrive at the courts is my 97-year-old mother, Minnie. People line up to get hugs from this remarkable woman. She competed in the National Senior Olympics in Birmingham, AL and took gold in the 90+ category. She even played singles. The medals she won are proudly displayed, right next to the video of her skydiving at age 88. Mom continues to play to this day.

Our daughter, Kristy, was a champion in platform tennis, and had a pickleball court in her backyard, well before this was common. When my grandchildren visit us in Michigan and Arizona, we make sure they get plenty of pickleball action. Introducing pickleball to our family is one of our greatest joys. We have helped cultivate the skills in a sport they can enjoy, even into their 90s.

Now in my 70s, I've accrued a fair number of honors throughout these decades. I was #1 singles in tennis at Western Michigan University. I hold national titles in pickleball, tennis, platform tennis and paddleball. I've been inducted into the Pickleball Hall of Fame, Platform Tennis Hall of Fame and the Huntsman World Senior Games Hall of Fame and The Kalamazoo College Hall of Fame as a coach. I'm also a founding member and director of the IPTPA, co-founder of the non-profit Pickleball Outreach, a certified pickleball referee, Pickleball Ambassador and co-tournament director for the annual Kalamazoo Pickleball Fever in the Zoo tournament.

Almost everything has changed since we discovered pickleball. It has greatly expanded our circle of friends, our Pickleball Family. We have traveled to places near and far through pickleball. In 2018 we went on our most memorable pickleball adventure to New Zealand. We stayed mostly in the homes of pickleball enthusiasts during our three-week visit. This afforded us the chance to experience first-hand the friendliness of the Kiwis. As a director of the IPTPA pickleball professional organization, we certified the first teaching professional in New Zealand. At that time pickleball was in its infancy in New Zealand. Most of the pickleball venues were in badminton halls. Memories of the places and people we saw there will always bring a smile. We have also gone on Audrey Phillips' Pickleball Adventures to various resorts in the Caribbean and Mexico.

Sharing all of these experiences with my husband Jim is priceless. Pickleball has greatly improved my life. I get to hang out and have fun with my family and friends. In addition to connecting with so many wonderful people, there's the mental part of the game and the physical conditioning that comes with pickleball. It's a sport for a lifetime.

Nicole Havlicek

From Injury to Success

It was October 2017 and I was getting ready to play in my first pickleball tournament which just so happened to be Nationals, one of the biggest tournaments of the year. I was excited, confident and looking forward to having a blast competing on a court again, something I hadn't done for 15 years since my days of playing collegiate tennis.

I had just discovered the joy of playing pickleball earlier that year and started playing regularly. Thanks to my Division 1 tennis background at the University of California, Berkeley, I was fortunate to be able to roll over many of my tennis skills into my pickleball game. I adapted them as needed and in a few months, I was playing at a pretty high level and I felt tournament ready.

Two weeks before the event, I was in the middle of an intense training session when I felt sharp pains in my hip and lower back. I tried to keep going but it was clear the pain wasn't going away. I had to stop training for the day. Everyone there thought I would be able to shake it off in a few days and be back at it but I had a bad feeling that this was a much bigger problem.

The truth is, I had been battling this injury since my days of playing college tennis. I had seen so many different specialists about it over the years and nobody could figure it out. Deciding to start playing pickleball and training for pickleball tournaments had clearly exacerbated the problem and ultimately my body broke down.

I had to apologize to my partners and pull out of the tournament. That was really difficult. It was clear I was going to have to hang up my pickleball paddle for some time and resolve this injury once and for all. This was going to be a massive undertaking because the doctors still weren't able to give me a diagnosis. I had to set out on my own journey to find the answer. I knew it was going to be a very long road.

Simple day-to-day functionality became more of a problem as well. I didn't know how long it was going to take to get normal functionality back. It could take months or even years. The timeline was totally unclear. This was the dark hole I was staring into. It was scary and unsettling to say the least.

Playing pickleball was out of the question but did that mean I had to be sidelined from the sport altogether? I took inventory of my skills and thought about how I could stay connected and help the sport grow while I recovered.

At the time, I was a tennis coach. During my career as a semi-professional tennis player, I never saw myself as a coach, but I started coaching by chance to help a friend and I learned I was pretty good at it and what's more… I really enjoyed it! I seem to have a knack for breaking things down in a systematic way and communicating it in a way people could understand and translate into their play.

I also love the internet. I had dabbled in a few internet businesses over the years. I knew how to make websites, film and edit videos, write copy, create graphics, do search engine optimization and all kinds of other online skills.

I combined my love for pickleball, my knack for coaching and my internet skills and co-founded a business focused on instructional content for pickleball players striving to become as good at the game as they can possibly be. We called it PrimeTime Pickleball and we focused our attention on YouTube. There were a few other YouTube channels in the space but there was definitely room for more content. In fact, our feeling was that the pickleball community was hungry for more content. In our view, video content was perfect for the task at hand because lots of demonstration was needed to get pickleball lessons across in the best possible way.

We started posting 1-2 videos per week on every topic we could think of that would help players get better at their game. Each covers one tip or a set of tips about a key aspect of the game: stroke technique, strategy, footwork, drills, how to train etc… At its core, pickleball is a simple game, but if you want to play it at a high level then there's a lot of nuance to master in many different aspects so there's a lot to cover.

The videos got a lot of views and attention early on. People really seemed to like what we were putting out there. As our video count and the game itself grew, so did the PrimeTime Pickleball Youtube channel. We added the primetimepickleball.com website so that we had yet another platform to reach people and share tips about this great game with them.

It became clear that as great as pickleball tips were, people wanted more in-depth content. Doubles was clearly of the most interest and it seemed like doubles strategy was a topic that many needed help with once they started to get the basics of strokes down. We knew we could help with that so we set out to create what we felt was the best and most comprehensive doubles strategy course on the market. We called it Dominating Doubles. It features 100+ step-by-step walkthrough video lessons of the best systematic way to play doubles pickleball so you can win more. The course, like the Youtube channel, was very well received.

In August 2021, my business partner and I decided to go our separate ways and I became the sole owner of the business. The growth just kept on going and in October of 2022, the YouTube channel crossed the 100K subscriber mark. The first channel to achieve that milestone. As proud as I am of that accomplishment, for me, it pales in comparison to what happened next.

As a thank you to our pickleball subscribers, we gave away 10 premium pickleball paddles with a custom design to commemorate the event of reaching this milestone. All one had to do to enter the contest was submit a funny story about pickleball or let us know how PrimeTime had helped them achieve their pickleball goals. There were hundreds of submissions and most of them were overflowing with stories, examples and gratitude about how PrimeTime had touched their lives in a positive way in pickleball and beyond. I was overwhelmed by the response.

If I'm ever frustrated when editing or struggling to come up with the right way to say something on any particular video, I go back to those stories and messages as well as the ones I regularly receive via email. I'm quickly reminded of why I do what I do and it gives me the strength to get my head right and figure things out so that I can keep helping people through this great game.

The truth is, if I can help people feel better about any area of their life, in this case pickleball, that joy overflows into other areas of their lives and by association, it touches their families and friend's lives in a positive way as well. That alone plus all the great connections and friendships I have made through pickleball is enough to keep me fired up and looking forward to doing this for many more years to come.

And, as counterintuitive as it may seem, I'll also be eternally grateful to pickleball for forcing me to finally stare down the injury that has been plaguing me my entire adult life. It's been an extremely long road and as it turns out, it has taken years, not months to work through.

I'm not totally out of the woods yet but I did finally solve the puzzle of what my injury is all about and am well down the road to recovery. I have learned so much about myself and my body in the process and in that way it has been an invaluable gift. That said, I can't wait to get past it and back on the court for gameplay again when the time is right.

Knikki Hernandez 

Pickleball, My New Home

Lost doesn't even begin to describe what I was feeling when I found pickleball. Trying to recover from my recent divorce, I did the only thing I knew to heal from the pain: I went to the basketball court. It's the one place in the world that gives me complete inner peace and makes me feel at home. In my early thirties, and newly divorced, my only focus was on mentally coping with my situation. I knew I could find some solace with a leather Wilson basketball. Each bounce, dribble, shot and rebound was the medicine that gradually restored my physical strength, and what followed, like a soda chaser to a tequila shot, was my mental fortitude.

Piece by piece, I began rebuilding the foundation of my life. When the days were particularly difficult, I would stay at the free-throw line for long stretches of time until I could regain focus and stability. Three dribbles to the right. One to the left. Spin. Shoot. Swish. One for One. This became my daily routine.

Then one day, a woman in her 60s headed towards the court as I stood watching her from the top of the key. I assumed that she would do some stretching and band work and then quickly depart. Then a man, about the same age, with a red, white, and blue headband put his bag down next to the bench. It was obvious these were not basketball players. However, they took over the court. Before I realized it, more and more people gathered on the court like birds migrating South for the winter. Who were these people? Soon they dominated the court.

Suddenly there was no more room for me to shoot hoops. Frustrated that I couldn't play basketball, but intrigued about what they were about to do, I walked up to one of the women and said, “Hi, I’m Knikki. Are you guys about to take a class?” “No,” she responded in an excited tone. “We’re about to play PICKLEBALL!” “Can I play?” I asked shyly, figuring if you can’t beat ‘em join ‘em. “Absolutely! Just grab a paddle from over there and sign up on the list.” I looked in the box with all the wooden paddles. Looks official, I thought. Before I stepped on the court, I watched four players play an entire match as one of the gentlemen explained the rules to me. Easy enough, I told myself.

Little did I know that these retirees would have me running wildly all over the court. To say that these people made me look out of shape would be the understatement of the century. They mopped the floor with me. Some of them were extremely agile and mobile. Most had quick hands and could put some lethal spin on the ball. My youth and mobility were no match for these players, and my ego couldn’t handle that. But it was just what I needed.

From that day forward, I looked forward to going to the gym but not to shoot around. I craved more pickleball. It was a different and uncharted territory. I had no paddle experience, no tennis background, and no understanding of a proper forehand. Not to mention I wasn't winning many games.

Truth be told, pickleball was far more humbling than my divorce. It didn't take long before pickleball started to feel like home. Following a difficult year of isolation, thanks to pickleball I connected with people again. Even more important than my love for competition, I have made true friends. Pickleball had given me a new place to land, a new place to call home. Basketball will always be my first love because it gives me Kobe-like confidence, however, pickleball has given me what I need most in my post-divorce life— joy.

Nancy Hosford

Back to Life Again

At eight years old I was a pretty good gymnast. But my spine prohibited me from pursuing the sport, as I had a severe case of scoliosis. Instead, when I was 10 I chose to play tennis. By the time I was 13 I had a spinal fusion. It was fairly archaic back then. I had to lay in bed for a week in traction to grow and straighten my spine prior to surgery. Amazingly, I grew three inches.

I continued playing tennis in my hometown of Delaware in high school. Then I played for the University of New Hampshire. I was one of the lucky ones who received a Title IX scholarship—one of the first girls to be a recipient. After beating a senior I ended up taking over the tennis team as a freshman and played number one singles. I had gone back and forth with tennis and field hockey, but now I was focused on tennis.

In collegeI had another spinal fusion, this time my cervical spine, from an accident at tennis camp. I dropped out of college my sophomore year. By the time I went back to school I was ok, but I was very weak. Eventually I was able to get my number one position back, but I could not manage singles and switched to playing doubles.

After college I moved to Boston and became a tennis pro. That's when I met a cute tennis pro named Matt, and together we headed West. By the time we hit Tucson, Arizona, we had run out of money. So that is where we stayed and married. I've lived in Tucson for 35 years now. I was a tennis pro at a resort in town for four years followed by a 25-year career in media—TV, radio and advertising.

The truth about tennis is that each time I have had physical adversity, it has pulled me back to life from the physical drama.

At 35 years old I was diagnosed with a rare strain of thyroid cancer which metastasized to my fused spine. This was right after having my daughter MacKenzie. I received a barbaric amount of radiation from chronic radiation surgery. This caused me to go directly into menopause. The stress on my marriage was palpable. Matt couldn't fix me and that pulled us apart. I just couldn't get well. We divorced. Our daughter went back and forth but soon I was too sick to take care of her and Matt had to come home to help us. I am so grateful that we had a second chance. We remarried.

I've learned a lot from this situation, mostly, it's best to search within your heart. We vowed to never let cancer come between us again. In 2011 I got embolisms from radiation. Five doctors said they didn't know how I was still alive. Once again I ended up in the ICU. I was in bed. I had pleurisy, weighed only 90 lbs and battled chronic pneumonia for years on breathing machines. I was not well and on a lot of medications. I got addicted to the drugs and one day I just flat out stopped all of the medications.

One night I had a miracle dream that changed my life. I dreamed I was getting re-certified as a tennis pro. When I awoke, I got out of bed and started hitting tennis balls for a few minutes a day. By 2018 I began to get some strength back and worked at the Country Club teaching. The pro, Joe Efarious, was teaching pickleball, he left the club and soon after I took over as the pro and learned the game. I was fortunate to learn from Helle Sparre, who taught me how to play. She was the perfect coach for me as she was also from tennis and now playing pickleball.

And then, I ended up with breast cancer. I had used up Western medicine. I needed to find alternative remedies. I now use an ozone machine and more holistic treatments. The cancer sidelined me, but no one knew that I was suffering. I just showed up and kept it to myself. Just as tennis has always brought me back to life, now it is pickleball that is my best medicine.

I started giving back. I quit being a pro and founded ALL IN Pickleball, a 501c3 non-profit to serve disadvantaged youth through the Boys and Girls Club. We partner with intermediary agencies. So far we have served 200 youth through the program. We give away prizes, paddles and balls and make it a fun place for kids to come. Gearbox signed a three-year contract to sponsor the program with paddles and balls and Taco Bell donated food for our fall event called the Jolly Dashers. The best feeling is hearing from the kids after they participate. My favorite so far was the day we gave a paddle to a young boy and he said “This is the best day of my life.” We call our program “The Pillars of Character” that we took from golf: respect, trust, kindness and perseverance.

Today I am responsible for 30 women on two different pickleball teams. We have a State League Team. I'm actually on three teams. I run a practice for two teams each week and I'm at the Boys and Girls Club weekly where I teach pickleball. The kids go through the program, graduate and get a Gearbox paddle, ball, bag and water bottle. We've graduated 100 kids so far.

We need to get our coaches certified. They are all volunteers. The goal is to eventually get an Executive Director. A lot of people are interested in using our formula and structure to do a similar program in their towns. If it can be boxed up, I would gladly go and help develop it wherever.

Today I am about positive health. I get up in the morning, meditate, do yoga and stretch. I have fifteen fused vertebrae. After the first three cancer surgeries I had to have all the discs in my neck fused. This means I have to take care to strengthen. I listen to Buddhist spiritual teachings, use an electro-magnetic bed, do push-ups to strengthen my core and use a foot massager. Then I go and have a latte.

I also use Acupuncture, get massages and sometimes go on silent retreats and spend time in my garden which I love. Back in the day, I was cancer. Anyone who knew me knew that I had cancer. Oh, there's Nancy… cancer. I was chronically sick for 30-plus years. Now I have rid myself of the label. I am no longer a patient, I am no longer that. At 66, I am a miracle to be alive and well. My passion is serving youth and playing pickleball. I wake up every day and live a life of health since I found pickleball.

In pickleball I can lose myself in a rally. I love the **Inner Game of Tennis** (Timothy Gallway)—the principles are true for pickleball. I live in that inner game. The quiet focus, being in the moment of now. I'm not afraid of the future or the past. I'm in this moment. In pickleball I teach people to stay in the state of knowing: ready, read, react. These are my life guides.

I still have to deal with physical issues. I still struggle. I had to have new teeth four times due to radiation. I've had 10 implants. There are many side effects that I have to pay attention to and address. I have no saliva glands—so I need water at all times to produce saliva for me. When I'm playing pickleball, however, I forget about all of this.

The fact that I was so good at tennis helps me to be able to rally with anyone. I got to play with Irina Tereschenko a few times, which was wonderful. At this place in my life, pickleball represents freedom. It means health. It is my lifeline.

Natalie Hughes 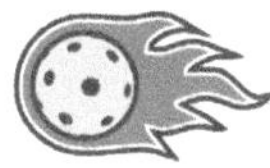

Peace in Pickleball

I'm so very fortunate to have found this silly pickle sport. I've also heard it called a cult and I have to laugh because I am always trying to get everyone to play, but it's for their own good.

I started playing pickleball on a random trip to Laramie, Wyoming, in order to escape the madness of living in downtown Denver, Colorado during the protests in 2020. My then partner and I were playing tennis every so often and had seen a solid pickleball crowd gathering and laughing later into the summer evenings. Our curiosity began brewing.

On that trip to Wyoming an old friend from my past reached out and told me she was living in the area. She didn't have time to meet but invited us to pickleball the next morning. It was really easy to play right from the start. People were giving us advice and excuses for why we were hitting bad shots. Then when we would hit a good one it seems like everyone on the courts would cheer for us. Of course I wondered if it was just these lovely Wyoming people that were so nice.

We went back to Colorado and bought a beginner pickleball set. The next weekend we went to a small pickleball tournament in Fort Collins. It was so cool. People showed up on bikes with snacks and music, tents and coolers. The day flew by and we met a bunch of great people that I still play with today. Soon we were spending a lot of time on the courts, meeting people from all walks of life, all ages and ethnicities, beliefs, income and ability levels. In spite of our differences, we had a lot in common. Where had these people been the last 20 years? I had never seen any of them before. I barely remembered the score of any of the games because I was having so much fun and exercising for hours at a time. Everyone has extra paddles and I would randomly invite anyone who was walking by or watching because it was most definitely my new favorite thing about life.

There are so many ways to win on the pickleball courts even when it's not about the score of the game. The jokes are flying, people are always sharing resources and invites to other events, and there are a billion fun(ny) ways to win and lose a point. It became a very addicting scene, most definitely the healthiest I had ever witnessed. It was flourishing all over Colorado.

In August 2020, my mom, Leslie, called and told me my grandmother received a terminal bladder cancer diagnosis with a six month timeline. She was 89 at the time and had lived one hell of a wild life. I don't know how else to describe her 90 years. She was a fun feisty soul all the way to the end. We were deeply saddened by the news. I received their blessings to come visit as often as I could. We spent a bunch of time together but my mom needed a distraction.

Mom agreed to come with me to the courts for some fresh air and hit the pickleball around. She has a lot of natural ping pong talent and quickly picked up the game. She started to take some snarky whippy shots at me (with smirks) and it was game on. We slowly crept into some games and people were very friendly without knowing our situation. She really needed this sort of instant easy community and kindness. It was a relief you cannot buy. We played for a few days, each day at a new set of courts. People continued to be very welcoming. It was beautiful and everything we needed.

What would become of that weekend together is beyond special. I couldn't be happier about the connectivity and continued joy pickleball provides her. She recently sent me a video of a garage band she checked out with her pickleball friends. How funny is that role reversal? She goes bike riding with her friends to lunch after pickleball. They go to concerts and celebrate birthdays together. She has definitely earned this lovely life she created.

One year after my Grandmother's departure, I was having a tough time at work and exiting my domestic partnership. My heart was shattered and I felt lost. I booked a trip to Mexico, a country full of appreciation and culture, to gather my thoughts. My mom came with me because she didn't want me to be alone. She found a lovely pickleball group in Puerto Morelos, Quintana Roo. I was chatting with one of the ladies when some young kids arrived with a soccer ball.

I asked if we could move one of our nets away from their goal and she obliged but told me the boys were probably hoping to be invited to play with us. I tried to hide my true reaction but bluntly asked, "You're not about to tell me you don't play with them?" She explained, "The kids are supposed to be in school but it's COVID so their schedules are off. We don't want to encourage this as an alternative to school and we don't have supplies for them to continue. Furthermore, people who are learning are unintentionally going to take away the limited resources of the expats and we don't have beginner materials." I asked, "So if we could get those things donated to the children would you play with them?" She said "Yes, absolutely!" I made a call and had everything donated in 10 minutes. I started playing a bit with the kids. They broke my mom's paddle in less than 10 minutes.

We put together a WhatsApp group and flew back down to teach and donate pickleball materials to the kids at the secondary school on April 3, 2022. It was far beyond anything I had ever imagined and so very impactful. The sports department of Quintanaroo came to learn and write about this and the expats now play regularly with the kids. Later in the year I went to La Cruz, in Mexico. I knew I wanted to bring pickleball materials so I started looking for the right people. A woman named Joan Gil came highly recommended by many people in the area. I reached out to her and got a feel for her needs. I decided to put it out to the local pickleball chapters that I would happily take their used gear down to Mexico.

I continued reaching out to different groups in the area of Puerto Vallarta. Each time I reached out for contacts I was given Joan's name. I was intrigued. My mom and I flew to Puerto Vallarta with six bags for a five-day visit. Joan is a force, altruistic in all her efforts, and a lifetime teacher from El Paso, TX, living in Mexico for more than 25 years.

The response was nothing short of overwhelming and inspiring. Chris Rossi, of InstaDink, single-handedly doubled my efforts and really opened the door to see what more we could offer these people. I picked up some materials from these local angels, and suddenly I had enough for more than three programs. When I gave Joan the materials she was kind of in shock. We spent some time playing with the kids and before we parted ways I told her I wanted to come back if we could have a bigger impact. “Nets, paddles, balls, wraps… What am I not thinking of?” “Shoes”, Joan replied. No problem, I thought! The more I put the pieces together the more I wanted to see how far my reach could go.

I arrived home on September 25, 2022. I filed nonprofit paperwork on September 29 and put together a pickleball tournament shoe drive for October 22. The response was beautiful and communal; even players who weren’t competing showed up to donate. November 25th, the day after Thanksgiving, I flew back down with six bags of shoes, nearly 80 pairs. We gave them to every player and their families and anyone who supported our efforts. Joan worked with local authorities to get approval to paint courts down in the harbor some time ago. The guards make sure the kids have priority use of the materials and courts. It’s those relationships and programs that have led me to feel this is where my time and energy should be full-time. This is where I feel most impactful and fulfilled so I have transitioned to make it my full-time priority.

I parted ways with a 10-year relationship with the alcohol industry in 2023. Last year I made over $170k. Luckily this afforded me the foundation to be able to pursue my passion and grow my newly established nonprofit, Peace in Pickleball. My organization seeks out people like Joan, the passionate boots on the ground, in order to grow the sport of pickleball by offering the resources necessary to incorporate it into local schools, youth, and family extracurricular programs.

Pickleball has paved the way for everything I love about my life. It’s emotionally, physically, mentally, & socially healthy and inspiring. It’s one of those rare, non-divisive things I feel brings connectivity and empathy to the world. I want to share it with everyone. My 10-year-old niece and nephew love it and so does my mom. That, in itself illustrates the range of inclusivity.

Shari Humes

You Go Girl

I created a bright pink T-shirt with "This Kitty Roars: Be Brave, Be Bold, Be Empowered", in response to a call for action for women's rights and a desire to empower women (and men) to honor and embrace their individuality and strength. I receive compliments whenever I wear my Kitty Roar shirt on the pickleball court. It is my desire to make a positive difference, to be the change I wish to see.

I found pickleball by supporting a friend who wanted to learn. I set her up with a paddle and swag. We played and I was hooked. I love how pickleball brings women together. Through my two-plus year journey playing, I have met the most wonderful, fun, interesting, athletic and intelligent group of women. This is such an unexpected blessing. My friends laugh at my pickleball life metaphors; my stamina to mow the lawn, walk the dog and then play two hours of pickleball. That's easy, pickleball is the fun part. My husband has become accustomed to later, more simple dinners and doesn't mind massaging my sore feet. Life is better with pickleball.

I started playing pickleball just before the COVID lockdown. I was already bitten by the pickleball bug, so playing outside in the cold and inside with a mask on was what kept me happy, fit, having fun and interacting with people. I remember the days of wearing a mask and foggy glasses and sweating under my mask—all for the love of pickleball.

One of my sayings is "I have to have fun, as much as a flower needs water." I also believe I make my own fun wherever I go. I chose to venture and play this addictive sport and feel alive in a new, healthy, vibrant way. I chose to be brave last year and take a trip to a pickleball camp in Oregon where I would not know anyone. I wanted to find out more about myself, push past limiting beliefs (am I too old, too slow, too something) and find new "I can do" beliefs. I wanted to learn new drills and skills I could take back home to "up" my game. I learned by watching the pros who were teaching: how to relax and have fun, not take each ball into the net or out of bounds so seriously. I learned how to do an Ernie. I met some amazing women who were generous, athletic and interesting. I realized I had a lot to learn. Most of all, I had fun.

Recently I lost my father, he was 92 years old. I miss his smile, his twinkly blue eyes, his gentleness and chivalry. Presently, I am traversing my brother's journey with Frontotemporal Dementia/ALS. He is only four years older than me. He is my bro. He is very sweet, loving and beginning to disappear. Pickleball has become my salvation. When I walk on the court for a lesson or to play a few games I find peace of mind focusing on the ball, my short game, laughing, being fully engaged and present. My mind is open to learning; I want to support my partner. I feel empowered when I let the angst fade away. When I tell my brother I am going to go play pickleball, he always says "You go girl!" I am going to miss that. I think I will take a video of him saying that to me. And perhaps when he is gone, I will start each game by saying to myself, "Ok, you go girl!"

I find in pickleball that mixed doubles is more of a power game. Men hit the ball harder and their strategies are different. I feel powerful resetting the ball, changing the pace and hitting a winner. This is all part of my learning to believe in myself, relax and play for the fun. Women's doubles I find has more finesse, along with hard drives. We even hit each other occasionally. But as we increase our skills we invite our partner's strengths to emerge and encourage teamwork.

There is no "I" in team. I cherish my pickleball ladies deeply. The strength, life experiences, how we hold space for one another, provide new opportunities, laugh deeply, play with passion, then go have a beer and share the rest of life. I am so glad I said yes to pickleball and yes to learning something new. I am brave, I am bold, and I am empowered and this kitty roars.

Sally Huss

Dare to Dink: Finding Pickleball

The Rocky Mountains, with its snow-covered Pikes Peak, loom above the fence line. Below sits an old tennis court—where dogs, kids on bikes and skaters are running freely through the pickleball players. The transformed court consists of painted lines, a sagging net and cracks with green grass sprouting through. New to the neighborhood, I was looking to meet new friends when I happened to wander over to check out the community park.

A group of middle-aged women was having the time of their lives—poking and pushing, smashing and slashing a whiffle ball around. I patiently watched trying to figure out the scoring structure and the point of the game. It was similar to tennis, however, they were playing on only a fraction of a full court. I was hoping that if I hung out long enough someone would see me and invite me to participate. When that moment arrived, I jumped in with a false confidence believing that I could play this game better than they could. After all, I had been the top junior tennis player in the country and a Wimbledon semi-finalist. This couldn't be that difficult, even at my age, 81. I quickly was schooled in just how much I needed to learn to master this sport.

Thus began my addiction to pickleball. Eventually, Those four women became my new best friends. In the following months we honed our skills and furthered our understanding of the complicated scoring system. I had recently joined a lovely resort nearby called The Garden of the Gods Resort and Club. They contracted me to teach my unusual form of tennis called "Zennis" – a happy, dance-like way of swinging at the ball and moving around the court. It wasn't long before I added pickleball to my teaching menu. Barely proficient at keeping score myself, I proceeded to teach others the basics of the game and tried to stay one step ahead of anyone I taught. The Head Rackets Pro was aghast when I told him that I had written and published a book on pickleball ***DARE TO DINK: Pickleball for Seniors and Anyone Else Who Wants to Have Fun.*** "But you've only been playing for six months!" he cried. I was undaunted, as I had previously written and illustrated over 100 children's books. I was eager to share what I had learned about pickleball.

To bolster my teaching, I began to migrate around town to the local public parks' pickleball courts. I watched, played, gathered new skills and made new friends. What I learned not only improved my own game, but helped me shed light on the breadth and depth of this sport to those I was teaching.

In gathering information for my book, I asked senior players why they liked pickleball and what it meant to them. Many were delighted to share their thoughts, including: "As a recent widow, and an empty nester, there is nothing like pickleball for making new friends, and having fun while exercising. If you don't take it too seriously, there is plenty of time for socializing." – Mary Kelley, age 63, level 2.5 (or maybe 2.0) "I love pickleball because of all the different people that I meet and enjoy who have this sport in common with me. Also, it is great exercise and good for the brain!" – Susan Brelsford, age 73, level 2.5

"Pickleball requires one to calculate angles and velocity faster than your opponents or be extremely lucky. Placement is more important than power or strength. Experience may serve you as much as talent or bravado. So, men do not have much advantage over skillful women, and age can play with youth, and size is less important than having excuses ready when you miss hit. Scoring is tough as it goes by ones rather than touchdowns or baskets. Celebratory dancing should be allowed." – Michael Chaussee, better known as Pancake, age unknown, level 2.0 or so (Authors note: Pancake is at least a 4.5 level player)

"We moved out here from Boston, Massachusetts so my partner of 47 years Josie could spend some time with her family. We felt that we were out of place here missing our friends from back home, our involvement with politics, our sports teams, our restaurants and yes, our community. On a bike ride we had seen this weird game being played down at Monument Valley Park, then they had a bit about it on the news. It sounded interesting as we both played tennis. We heard that the Westside Community Center gave lessons so we went to learn the game. Josie still plays at Westside and I venture over to MVP and join the community there. Now, 9 medals later we are both still playing the game."

We haven't given up our golf clubs and bowling balls, but the dust has accumulated on the tennis rackets." – Helen aka Boston McChesney, age

68, level 4.0 "What I love about pickleball is it's like I get to be a kid again! I haven't felt this way since competitive sports in high school!" – Mic Davis, age 69, level 4.0. My favorite comment came from the mother of a friend of mine: "The hardest part about playing pickleball is learning the names of all of my new friends!" – Pat Treacy, age 80, level 3.5 Although my book was aimed at seniors, I realized the essence of their comments would apply to any age.

As I continued my exploration into this sport, I made some very interesting observations. I learned that many beginners do not wish to be competitive. They just want to have fun. Then, as they progress in the sport by mastering certain shots and acquiring more skills, they begin to add a little competitiveness to their play. The better they get, the better they want to get. Some seriousness and greater focus creep into their play as they improve. Although pickleball can be played almost exclusively as "non-competitive", it still has the option for anyone who wants the opportunity to compete.

My own play has improved through the months with the addition of spins and slices, better ball control and touch. I find myself eager to learn more, such as–mastering court coverage, teamwork, the finesse of drops, etc. Even though pickleball appears to be a simple sport that anyone can play, it does require skill and focus. Players and teachers alike benefit by watching videos on YouTube and other social media channels. There's something for everyone at every level.

As an observer to the sport, I am encouraged by some of pickleball's basic truths: Gender and age make no difference in this game. Women and men play with each other equally, just as young play with old. Everyone is a teacher. If you don't know what to do or where to go on the court, someone will tell you. There is no class distinction. Only skill and enjoyment count. It's cheap! A handful of balls, a paddle and sneakers and you're ready.

I cannot quantify just how much pickleball has added to my life. As a senior woman, who was once a tennis champion, I am grateful at this stage in life that I am able to learn something new. As I improve I am able to share those strides in my teaching. This is a huge gift. I see it in my students, who are mostly senior players. One woman with two hip replacements had to give up riding horses. She is eager to learn pickleball and delighted with her progress, even designing her life around her new-found sport. It gives her something to look forward to and the prospect of meeting new people.

Teaching students who have never played before, never hit a ball of any kind before and are now discovering this sport and joining in groups, is one of the best thrills for me. My happiest times are the summers here in Colorado Springs when I can take my pickleball bag, a jug of water, visor and head to the courts at Monument Valley Park. Walking from the parking lot to the courts, through the big trees, my anticipation builds for what might happen and whom I might see. As I get closer and then walk the lanes of the courts, I hear, "Hi, Sally." "Hi, Sally." "Hi, Sally." "Good to see you, Sally." "Want to play in?" It makes my heart sing!

Courtney Jenkins

It All Starts With a Dream

I first grabbed a free wooden paddle out of the bin at Bender fields in Lynden, Washington in 2020. As a working, single mom, I was trying to figure out how to balance everything in my life. I had given up soccer due to the pandemic. That was when I learned about pickleball. It immediately became my passion. Who knew the sound of a holey yellow plastic ball would someday mimic the sound of my heartbeat.

The joy of learning a new sport and acquiring new skills grabbed me by my handle and took a deep grip of my heart. My face was masked, but my eyes and heart were wide open with adrenaline feeding my new addiction. The social aspect of meeting a new community of people who, like me, were starving for connection, filled me up. Everyone was so inviting. And it allowed me to stay in shape when I couldn't go to the gym. It was so nice to be outdoors and with others yet still be within safe distance of each other.

We played like addicts, constantly craving the next fix, and couldn't bear it when it rained. But of course there were squeegees and towels and the downpour wasn't stopping us. We groaned on days we couldn't go out and dreamed up ways to play inside. We bartered for time in gyms and settled graciously for yellow tape on wood floors. Our hearts were happy again, but we wanted more. We wondered how we could take these desires and make them real and have a place to play inside.

That's when I met Craig Cooper. He shared my same dream of opening an indoor pickleball facility. He had been soliciting the community for a good partner to brainstorm and rally the community. Craig tenaciously pursued the owners of the 1910-built old National Guard fortress—the Armory in Bellingham,WA. This task alone took many weeks for a response. The building was perfect. The idea was grand. The ceilings were lofty—just like our dreams for indoor play. The mammoth wood beams sculpted the architecture as if it was built for the game, before it was even a thought.

In five months, the 8600 square foot slab housing five courts paved the way to our dream coming true and I found a way to dig in. Once an Armory housing guns and a rifle range, then a roller skating venue for 20+ years, this castle-like fortress of a building, would make history again: The birth of Armory Pickleball.

Blood, sweat of tears were poured into the project, on top of our full-time jobs and now this "historic house of pickleball" in Whatcom County, has encouraged, inspired and opened its doors and the hearts of our members, old and new. They come and they smile and we have brought life and the ability to share our sport with like-minded players. A place to share our passion and find friends and as a way out of the pandemic, together.

As the co-owner of what I think is one of the coolest pickleball facilities in the Pacific Northwest, I feel as though pickleball is a marriage—I married my best friend. And the facility is a yearlong dream come true. We worked with the building owner on tenant improvements, tons of painting old walls and refinishing the original maple floors that surround the courts and in the entryway. On top of our full-time jobs, we made this happen with the help of others.

It is now being run as a keyless entry membership-based high-class pickleball facility. My heart is full, my head ready to explode at times, with challenges and excitement and new ideas every day that come from us and our members and a community that supports us. Our community is what makes the whole project worthwhile.

I think about this marriage and dream come true:something old— the 1910 Armory building something new—our amazing community; something borrowed—historical memories of this building: something blue—the courts. I can't believe it, even though I felt it every step of the way and every piece of clothing I ruined with paint or breathed in the dust or fumes. It has been a labor of love to finally open. My journey is not long, but my love for this sport is now deep.

We are starting "Pickled Pink", a women-inspired program to enable the runway for women in pickleball. We will be hosting pickleball clinics and conventions and ladies' gatherings at the Armory. We will be starting a foundation for youth pickleball and add more diversity to our community. These are things I feel strongly about and other women in our membership do as well. We have found a new third place and we are thriving.

We recently were nominated for Whatcom County small business start-up of the year. We were very honored by the nomination. We are featured in **Business Pulse** magazine and **In Pickleball** magazine.

As a woman, I feel empowered to share my journey with others, to encourage them to dig in and do more for our sport and for our communities. It just takes some vision, some determination and a lot of hard work.

CJ Johnson

The Many Faces of Influence

My dear friend Bev is the type of friend that when she asks you to do something you just show up. So that day when she invited me to play something called pickleball, I showed up. Like many players, I quickly fell in love with the game.

Athletics has always been a part of me. I grew up at a time when girls weren't always allowed to play sports. However, Mom was an athlete with a passion for skiing and golf. In one of my favorite pictures, she's holding a pair of skis that tower a good foot above her petite 5'2" frame and smiling ear to ear. Dad had the same passion. He was so anxious to get me on a pair of skis that he and his friend built a special backpack to get me on the hill, even though my little legs weren't quite ready. He was so excited until he made his first turn to the left, and he could feel the forces of the turn continuing to push me farther away. You would think the experiment would have ended, but no. He went back to the drawing board and built a more stable backpack. I had skis on my feet before my second birthday. I swear that's why I still trip so much. I had golf clubs in my hands before I was five.

I guess it was natural that I would grow up to be a professional athlete and find a way to make a living out of playing. My favorite memory of my Grandpa Ernie was his confident smile when he hit his first and only hole-in-one. I looked at him and said, "Grandpa, I think it's in the hole," to which he responded, "I know it is." Despite being a time when there was little money in the sport, and the road was daunting at best, he encouraged me to pursue a career as a golf professional.

Looking back, I realize there are numerous people who have influenced me along the way. Both men and women have had tremendous impacts on my life in athletics. Being a woman in athletics has presented challenges many times. My male business partner and I were teaching a pickleball camp at my local club. We were at the courts with two other players getting in a few games. At the end of our games, unbeknownst to me, one of our local players challenged him in a schoolyard sort of way that would have left me out of the game to sit on the sidelines as a spectator. Calmly without incident, he politely refused the challenge. It left me wondering how many times someone stuck up for me.

My husband, a fellow golf professional, has always encouraged me to fight for my place at the table. He stood beside me when I needed support and held me when I wanted to let it all out. He has seen firsthand how difficult it is to be a woman in the male-dominated sport of golf.

I've come to appreciate that there are men out there who support and empower women. There are also many women who go out of their way for other women.

As a golf professional, I was fortunate to get an award from the LPGA (Ladies Professional Golf Association), the same year the association's founders were recognized. The evening before the main event there was a small private dinner for award winners and their guests. Here I was surrounded by the legends of the game, the women who started it all.

I sat in awe as the women shared their memories of the early days of the tour. One particular story stuck with me. At every tournament one of their responsibilities was to promote the event to the locals. One time, they were invited to tell their story between rounds of a boxing match. They laughed as they recalled sitting in the front row watching the fight until it was time for them to speak. Until I heard this story, I never knew one of the hazards of sitting in the front row was that the fighter's body fluids don't stay inside the ring. When they stood to speak, their Sunday best dresses looked less than stellar.

Another story from that same evening touched my soul in a much different way. I complimented one of the founders on her beautiful blouse. Her eyes lit up, and she thanked me. Her smile was quickly replaced by a sense of worry. She whispered softly in my ear that it was the same blouse she'd worn to a celebration held just a few months previously. She was worried that people would recognize it, but she couldn't afford anything new. Here I was making a lucrative living in the sport where she paved the way, and she couldn't afford a new blouse.

These stories have taught me never to forget those who have come before me.There was the hospital executive, well into her 60s at the time, who had never played a sport, and didn't have an athletic bone in her body. She applied the same dogged determination that she used in her career to learn the game of golf to keep up with her male counterparts.

Neither the Associate Dean of Students nor the Athletic Director from a D3 university system school (both women) were particularly fond of golf, but every year they put aside their egos and spent a long day on the course with me at a charity event. They were there to support a young man they had taken under their wing when he was a struggling student-athlete, an inner-city kid who went to a lily-white state college to play basketball. He was the first to tell you that he would have never made it through school and eventually into the NBA without the support of the women in his life. Those ladies showed me that taking time to empower another person is perhaps the most important thing we can do.

There have been many roadblocks in my journey. The time I was the only woman playing in a men's golf event—I was frequently the only girl—however this event was different. The sponsors set up free food and drink for all the participants. That was a treat when you were a young starving golf pro. When I finished my round, I stopped in the golf shop to get directions to the event. After following the instructions through a twisted maze of hallways in the massive clubhouse, imagine my shock, embarrassment, and anger as I stood outside the entrance to the men's locker room.

That experience, and many similar ones, were the impetus for me to spend nearly 20 years of my golf career as a volunteer board member in two different sections of the PGA. I wanted to make sure that other young women were given equal opportunities.

And now, there’s pickleball. It didn’t take me long to realize that the advice I was getting at the court was questionable at best. I started playing before the pickleball boom so there weren’t any coaches locally and there was a limited amount of information available online. As a lifelong athlete and coach, I knew that meant I had to become a student of the game. I consumed everything I could find and there was a lot of trial and error.

I was so frustrated by the incorrect advice that one day I turned on a camera, talked about it and posted it to YouTube. That’s how the Better Pickleball Channel was born. Fast forward several years I became co-founder of WeArePickleball. My partner Tony Roig and I publish the largest suite of pickleball instructional content available including two YouTube channels, a podcast, weekly blog and the Pickleball Summit.

Today, when I'm out on the courts, I see some women who weren't allowed to play sports as young girls, laughing, making friends, and having the time of their lives. That's what sports have always been for me. Friends, fun, and a way to find out more about who I am as a human being. It's not just about the sport. It's about the things that playing the sport teaches you about yourself.

So many people have informed me, walked alongside me, or come after me, that have empowered me not just to be the athlete that I am, but the self-confident woman I learned to be. Whenever I'm getting ready to coach pickleball, I take a breath and recall one of the first lessons I received while pursuing my golf certification. A world-class instructor stood at the front of the room of more than 500 young golf pros and said, “if you don't remember anything I'm about to teach you regarding the golf swing, you need to remember this. The person is always more important than the golf swing.”

He was right. I didn't remember anything else he said, but here I am more than 30 years later, and I still remember that the person is always more important than the game. To me, that's what empowerment is all about.

Arathi Kashipathi

Cyber Ninja by Day, Whiffleball Wacker by Night

I am a wife (to an amazingly supportive husband), mother (to two beautiful girls), a computer engineer by education, a cybersecurity specialist by profession and a full-time pickleball fanatic, by choice. While growing up in India, sports had always been a big part of my life. I played tennis at the state level and softball at the national level during my high school/college years and won the national championship twice. When I was headed for the national championship for the third time, I fell ill and was diagnosed with acute nephritis and hospitalized. It was during this period that I realized how much I loved sports and what I was missing. It is said that "Health is a crown that the healthy wear, but only the sick can see." I remember the hollow feeling of lying on the hospital bed and vowed that once I recuperated, I shall do everything I can to stay healthy and fit. True to my word, since then, health and fitness have been a big part of my subconscious.

After moving to the United States, I played in the USTA league for a few years until motherhood and my profession eclipsed my schedule. I switched to running and quenched my adrenaline thirst with 10ks and half marathons. I turned into a gym rat and started enjoying various activities like strength training, cycling, Zumba and yoga. During a chance encounter at the company water cooler with two colleagues, I overheard the word pickleball for the first time. Curiosity got the better of me and I asked my colleague to tell me what it was. Being a lifetime sports enthusiast, I wanted to check it out and we quickly set up a time to meet at the local YMCA.

There were no outdoor courts in the area and the Y was the only refuge. He explained a few basic things, hit the ball a few times with a wooden paddle and we quickly got into a game, as playing was the easiest way to learn the rules. I remember thinking that it was fun, and I would explore it again as time permitted. Little did I know that I had been exposed to an addictive game and it would soon take over all my free time, and yes, even my life.

It was right around the time when we became empty nesters. Both of our girls started their college journey and the memories of the fun pickleball game came back. It couldn't have come at a better time. Initially, I started playing once a week as a filler for my regular gym workout. Gradually, the frequency increased, and my other gym workouts took a backseat. Before long, I played regularly, took some clinics and even a boot camp with the Pickleball Guru. Soon after, pickleball became my solace and my addiction. I started traveling for tournaments all along the East Coast and the South and have a private wall of medals to boast.

I have met amazing people from all walks of life and all age groups. Thanks to pickleball, I have friends from eight to 80 years old, from construction workers to CEOs and from various corners of the world. I would have neither crossed paths with many of them nor had great friendships with them, had it not been for pickleball.

We did a girls' trip to Florida and spent a week enjoying each other's company and competition. Before long, my husband and our daughters also started playing and now pickleball has become the family's game of choice whenever the girls come home from college and want to do a family activity. The girls are waiting for a day when they can beat their mom, but in the meantime, I am enjoying my reign.

Just as our county built outdoor courts, COVID arrived on the world stage. I was already bitten by the pickleball bug by then. So, we nailed up a few baseboards in the garage and started using the garage wall for drills and workouts shared on Facebook by professionals and enthusiasts. When the total ban was relaxed, we started playing outdoors again, initially only with family and gradually with limited friends. I remember those days of dunking the balls in Clorox water, wearing gloves & masks for playing & hand sanitizing after every game. The COVID years would not have been the same or emotionally manageable without pickleball.

The pickleball court is my favorite "third place" to be. It is a fun, neutral place with no obligation for attendance, membership, or purchase, to play with whoever and as long as one wants (after following basic court etiquette), play competitive or recreational games and spend time with friends. One of the many good things about the game is that in most places, you can just show up and play. No need for elaborate scheduling, planning or commitment. At the end of a long day at work, I look forward to whacking the whiffle ball at the nearby courts. It helps me de-stress, bask under the sun & breathe in the fresh air, quench my competitive spirit, and enjoy the camaraderie of friends. I couldn't ask for more.

Bonnie Koch

Giving Back and Paying Forward

A significant injury sidelined me during my tenure as a physical education teacher at a high school in Colorado. I coached high school volleyball and then was the head coach at Colorado Mesa University for the Women's Fast Pitch Softball program. Due to the injury, I was no longer able to teach or coach, but knew in my heart of hearts that I wanted to be around education and kids.

Through the process of my rehab from my injury, I worked with an Occupational Therapist and we talked about my need to change professions. She suggested I look into becoming an OT at the school setting. That would be a way for me to continue to be involved in the educational milieu. I was accepted into OT school and graduated with a BS in Occupational Therapy.

I worked in this capacity until my retirement. At the time of my retirement I realized I wasn't ready to retire and went on to work as a contracting OT in Hawaii and then in Arizona. I felt I had a lot to share through the occupational therapy process by becoming a strong advocate for parents with special needs children. After five full years of contracting my services, I retired for good.

Upon retirement for the second time, I retreated into a deep and dark place. I literally sat on my couch for a month and watched TV. I was immobilized by a persistent depression; feeling that I had lost my purpose in life. I was very worried about myself and how I had mentally deteriorated. As a strong, capable and always in control woman, I knew I had to keep this to myself for fear others would judge me. My own negative opinion of myself was significant. So I told no one and acted as if I was happy and didn't have a care in the world.

I carried around my sadness. I wasn't sure what was going to happen next. Eventually, I sought out a mental health provider to help guide me in finding my purpose again. In an effort to get me out of the house, a friend invited me to come to watch her play at the USA Pickleball National Tournament in Arizona. Since I was still putting on a happy face, I agreed to meet her there. After that introduction to the sport, I was very curious and asked my pal to teach me how to play. This was the medicine I needed to help with my mind-numbing depression.

My friend took me to her courts and showed me the game. I quickly became a regular player and noticed a significant change in my mood and my outlook. Pickleball was now becoming a life focus; one in which I could ask as a teacher/mentor and had an outlet for my competitive nature. I realized then that the game of pickleball gives retired people a new sense of meaning and purpose in their lives.

While I had let all of my credentialing expire as a teacher and as an OT that loss of identity was difficult to accept. It was at this point that I pursued certification as an instructor with the International Pickleball Teaching Professional Association(IPTPA) - Level II and as a certified coach with Helle Sparre's Dynamite Doubles.

Pickleball has taken me from the depths of despair and feeling like I no longer had a purpose in life, to being able to rediscover myself. It has been a beautiful journey back into a meaningful life. Today I am playing at the 4.0 level. I also teamed up with another player from my community and we have written our own curriculum geared at retirees. I live half the year in AZ and half in Colorado and am certified to teach in both states.

I have come to learn that there isn't anything worse than not having a sense of purpose. I affirm the positives that have enveloped me in pickleball: I am a good teacher, people ask to take lessons from me and I am appreciated for my kindness, gentleness and ability to differentiate instruction by assessing my students' needs and abilities.

I have also done some contract work with pickleballtournaments.com as a desk operator and registration coordinator. During this work I have been able to guide beginning tournament players through the challenging process of registering for their first tournament, calm their nerves and positively support their journey into the world of tournament play.

The highlight of my pickleball journey so far is having worked with Rob Davidson in his pickleball camps and working with Helle Sparre. These are two of the most amazing players and human beings in the world of pickleball!!

Although I am not currently playing tournaments, I continue to be a student of the game and a teacher. Looking for a partner who is a good fit for my strategies and style has been a journey! Let's face it, we all approach the game differently. Pickleball has a unique smattering of all sorts of personalities! There are those in it for the pure pleasure and socialization and those who want to win at all costs. I have had my share of playing against folks who were only looking for the "W" and those are the folks that I smile at - say "thank you" and move on to another court. I will kill them with kindness for sure!!

I am excited to be giving back to the community. I am traveling as an instructor to Bhutan in August, 2023 with Dotti Berry, Helle Sparre and others. We will be working with a head coach in a sports area in Paro. There will be a process of teaching new coaches, certifying those who are interested in taking pickleball to the next level and introducing pickleball to a foreign country. Bhutan wants to grow its sports programs for their youth and their communities. This is an amazing opportunity and supports my purpose and pays my experiences forward. I can't imagine that I could have done any of this without pickleball in my life.

I am fortunate to have my mom (88) as my biggest cheerleader. While she has macular degeneration and has trouble seeing the ball, she comes to cheer for me when I play. "I can't always see you, but I can hear the ball and all of your friends laughing and I enjoy that more than anything."

Joanna Laubscher

Thank You Pickleball

Just before COVID hit, I joined a friend of mine on a trip to the local recreation center. She was going to check out pickleball, and I had been wanting to try it for a couple of years, so I was excited to finally give it a go. My life up until then had been full of travel for work, kids, and a wife and there seemed to be no time for anything else. I had been in the grind of running from one to the next. Lucky for me, they were all things more than worth running for, but deep down, I felt like this wonderful life of mine was missing a piece.

I grew up playing competitive sports and continued sports through high school and college. It didn't matter what the game was, I was good at it and I loved it. Sports were my happy place, and when I played in my last competitive softball game, my heart broke. I cried in the dugout knowing that it would be next to impossible to find something that I was that passionate about and to be surrounded by people that shared that passion with me. As I moved on in life, I stayed active. I spent more time running or on my bike, but nothing ever filled that void of playing sports. So, I was excited to walk into that gym on a cold, snowy January morning to try this silly game. My friend handed me a paddle and without even hitting a ball, I looked at the paddle and said, "Oh dear, my life is forever changed."

Only a few weeks later the world flipped upside down and we were no longer allowed to go to the recreation centers to play. Lucky for us Coloradans, we had a warm spring so I started playing outdoors regularly with a group of guys. For the first time in my adult life, I wasn't on a plane all the time for work. In a stretch that COVID made so scary, I almost felt guilty because I was so happy. I was able to be home with my family, and I had the time to do a sport that I had grown to love so much.

I played as much as I possibly could. As a former athlete, I could feel the passion build. I just wanted to do whatever it took to get better. I felt like a kid again. I started getting invited to an amazing group of players, and my game continued to improve. I made new friends, and a new chapter in my life began.

I had been on the Marketing Team at New Belgium Brewing for ten years when I found pickleball. I immediately recognized the pickleball community to be friendly, inclusive, loyal and very social. I also noticed the tendency to sit around and enjoy a cold one after playing. I recognized the opportunity as a beer brand to engage with this demographic, so I built a three-year brand strategy and pitched it to our CMO. I was given the go and things just snowballed.

Over the next couple of years, I made it a point to learn as much about the sport, the leagues, the tours and understand the way pickleballers think. I met as many people as I could, and I implemented the brand plans I had devised. As a player and a fan, it was a little surreal to be combining my worlds and finding myself in places like the floor of the New York Stock Exchange for a Major League Pickleball event. I mean, let's be honest, that was really unbelievable. I was genuinely proud to be ahead of the craze and bring a national, well-known beer company to a sport that most of the world wasn't taking too seriously.

Things have changed quite a bit since 2020, and the playing field for tours and sponsors and investors has evolved quickly. While challenging, it's been a fun ride trying to keep up with the business of pickleball and figure out how our brewery can best support the sport and engage with players. However, there is one thing that has not changed for anyone, no matter who you are, and that is the joy of being on the court and spending time with friends. A person can walk by any court at any time of day and see people out there running and jumping and laughing. It's impossible not to see how much happiness pickleball brings to people.

There is no doubt in my mind that pickleball saved me. And while I know I'm not alone is this feeling; I know that everyone's story is unique. I needed something for myself. I had been looking for so many years for something that excited me. I had no idea how my life would change that day in January, but I knew it would. Deep down, I craved new friends that didn't live across the country. I missed feeling like I was a part of something. In the past three years, I have met some of the most wonderful people. I have made friends from entirely different backgrounds and different ages. I have connected with people I never would have met if it weren't for pickleball.

As I write this on a chilly February morning, I can hear the birds chirping outside. It's the first day I've heard them this year and it brings a smile to my face. I've always loved spring; it reminds me of the first days of softball practice when I was younger. I grew up in Chicago where the second it hit forty degrees, we were running around in shorts and t-shirts. We'd practice in the mud, and I would go home at night and tell my mom about my day, how I practiced and what games were on the schedule for the season. It still warms my heart to think about those evenings. Now thirty years later, I'll bundle up a little bit, find an empty court that might still have a little snow on the sidelines, play until it gets dark, and maybe grab a beer with my friends. After that, I'll go home, kiss my wife, and tell her about how much fun it was. And for that I say to pickleball, thank you.

Debbie Lawrance 

Ability with a Disability

I was just walking by when I saw two people playing a sport I didn't recognize. I asked them what they were doing. They explained it was called pickleball. They invited me to come the following day to give it a try. Curious, I showed up. I felt like a schoolgirl—they all looked like they played well, knew each other and were having a good time. It was an odd situation at my age that I would feel so intimidated. Me, of all people. I had run for public office, campaigned and had no problem being "out there." But for some reason, this situation caused me to feel anxious and uncertain.

The awkwardness reminded me of how it feels at the beginning of something new. Soon after, I was looking to play and was told emphatically by another woman that I was unwelcome as a beginner. Fortunately, a kind couple overheard and welcomed me on the court with them. This act of kindness was very empowering and encouraging and got me on my path to finding my way in pickleball. I am often reminded of this gesture and pay it back as much as possible so others can feel that inclusiveness.

That kindness has prompted me to teach kids, beginners, organize ladies' and mens' nights in addition to a new fun event we call musical night. We typically see 30-40 people show up for this night. People are randomly paired and play for fifteen minutes until the whistle blows and they change partners. The beauty is that we welcome all ages and all skill levels. I also help facilitate tournaments for those strong players who want to compete.

I eventually earned my coach's certification and have been working hard to get tennis courts converted and dedicated to the much-needed demand for pickleball courts. I addressed our group's desire to the Mayor and City Council with a formal presentation. I arrived at City Hall stressed out but nailed the presentation.

We received a unanimous vote in our favor. Everyone in attendance clapped with joy after the vote. As I stood up, I realized I had an intense headache. I smiled at the audience and said I needed to go home. Suddenly, everything went fuzzy. My wife, Irma (29 years together), took me to the hospital where they found I had a brain bleed. It lasted 6 hours as a misdiagnosed migraine. Similar to an aneurysm, I experienced a hemorrhagic stroke while at the local hospital. They transferred me to a major hospital where I was unable to speak or walk for approximately a week due to the large brain bleed.

After three weeks of recovery at home, Irma insisted I needed to get back on the pickleball court. I protested that my vision fields were impaired and it was unlikely I could manage to play. Irma was not taking no for an answer and continued to push me out the door. I eventually acquiesced and off I went to play. The minute I stepped on the court I knew I was in the right place. It felt so good and made me so happy to be there. It almost felt as if nothing in my life had changed. A few weeks later I was back into regular play days. I had to train myself to play with the vision disability and compensate with my other abilities. With only 80% of field vision, my expectations were low, but my enjoyment continued to be high. I wear protective eyewear and limit myself to rec play.

The pickleball community astonished me with their warmth and abundance of love and support. They rallied around me, brought me meals and showed up in a way that nourished my soul. As I look back, I realize how many positives have resulted since this incident. It is the common thread of an active lifestyle and the uniqueness of those I've met in the pickleball community. I am very grateful to Irma, my pickleball friends and the fact that I can still go out there and find happiness.

Elise Lehrfeld

Catching the Bug

It was a rough start. I was looking to find something both social and physical to do. In scanning our local township rec catalog in 2018, I saw a beginner class for something called pickleball. I did a quick Google search and decided this would be perfect for me, although I had never played any type of sport. I was excited to begin a new and exciting venture. However, the instructor criticized most of the students, including me. She even went as far as to tell us what to eat, because she had recently lost 20 lbs. She thought some of us could stand to lose a few pounds. Admittedly, I was a bit sensitive, having never played sports growing up. But having an instructor ridicule my attempts at serving and returning the ball really took a mental toll on me. On the last day of class I actually walked off the court in tears and decided pickleball was not for me. A few days later I decided to contact my township and let them know what had transpired during the class. It was no surprise that I was not the only person to complain about how we were treated.

My husband, Larry suggested I give it another try with a different instructor. I'm grateful that I followed his advice, and soon after fell in love with the sport. Kudos, to Larry, for his encouragement. Unfortunately, I was still working and was not able to play very often. I was lucky if I played twice a month for a couple of years.

Then, in March of 2020, I contracted COVID and was truly down and out for about six months. By September, when I started feeling a little stronger, Larry thoughtfully asked me what he could do to help me get back on my feet. I grabbed my pickleball paddle and said, "Let's go to the courts." Larry never wanted to learn to play pickleball. Yet, he selflessly went with me to help me heal. We started hitting the ball back and forth in order for me to regain confidence and get my lungs feeling better. This went on almost every day for about six months. I was still very short of breath and was only able to play for fifteen minutes a day before exhaustion took over. Although I was disappointed in my breathing situation, I pushed myself each and every time in order to get my stamina back. As the saying goes, if you want something bad enough, go for it!

During our time on the courts, I noticed Larry began inquiring about the rules, where to stand and how to serve. I wondered if he was beginning to get interested in pickleball. I was happy that my illness led him to the sport. Maybe this was the silver lining of being sick with COVID. Remarkably, not long after, he ordered a paddle and started watching pickleball educational videos. A couple of friends offered to play mixed doubles with us to help give us a better understanding of the game. I was still working part-time. So, while I was at work (thinking about pickleball), Larry started playing with friends and soon he too fell in love with the game. I was so happy for him, but I must admit that I was also a bit jealous. I was playing at most six hours a week and Larry was up to four hours a day. The friendly nature of pickleball was evident while playing at our local courts. I met a wonderful group of ladies who played together daily. They warmly welcomed me into their group and mentored me. They were very patient and encouraging as they taught me the finer points of the game.

I finally retired on April 1, 2022. I was invited to a party to welcome back some winter snowbird friends from Florida. At the gathering I was gabbing and laughing when my friend Marie said, “You know this party is for YOU.” My pickleball friends were thrilled that I had retired and surprised me with a party to celebrate. I have been told I am not a very observant person and now I know it is true. I looked around and realized there were happy retirement balloons, a cake saying happy retirement and there were pickleball decorations saying happy retirement. I was so overwhelmed that I actually started to cry. I truly love my pickleball ladies.

I have met so many wonderful caring people. Others may call them friends, but I call them my pickleball family. When a couple gets married and they vow for better or worse in sickness and health, this is how I feel about my pickleball family. We are always there for each other no matter what the situation is. Life has its ups and downs and we all go through some rough times. There are times I may be down and feel I should probably not play pickleball, but I force myself to go.

When I get to the courts, see my friends, and hear the wonderful sound of the pickleball hitting the paddle it’s like music to my ears. That’s when I know that I am in my happy place. This past November, two members of my pickleball family were registered to play in a tournament in Palm Beach Gardens, Florida. They asked me and two other friends if we would like to play in the tournament. I immediately declined saying I only participate in rec play. I am aware of my limitations. The three of us went to Florida in support of our friends who were playing in doubles 3.0. Although their outcome was a little disappointing, we had so much fun hanging out and laughing for the entire week together. The memories we made will last a lifetime. I've decided that if the same opportunity is available next November I will try to step out of my comfort zone and play in the tournament.

During this past summer our son also started to show an interest in pickleball. He lives in Cherry Hill, NJ and had a free Saturday with no plans. We invited him to our meetup in Horsham, PA to watch and possibly play a few games with our group. When he arrived and saw the level of play he said no way would he go onto the courts and embarrass himself. Larry and I continued playing and I noticed he made his way to the courts and was having a good time. Our friends were welcoming, showing him the ins and outs of the game. Now he loves the game as much as we do. He recently signed up for the Luck of the Draw round-robin tournament in South Jersey at Moorestown Tennis Club. I was skeptical about his choice. Lo and behold, he won a silver medal. We are so very proud and happy for him. Nowadays most of our conversations revolve around pickleball. At times he even asks for our advice on strategies.

Pickleball is a unique sport in the fact that all ages can play, it is physical, it's mental, it's social and it is emotional. The welcoming inclusivity of the sport means you can show up alone, as I did, with no sports background, and leave a few hours later with new friends and a love for a sport with a rather unusual name. COVID has changed so many lives in so many ways, but for me it was a blessing in disguise. We all know that COVID is contagious but believe me when I say Pickleball is contagious —once you start you can't help but catch the bug.

Sarah Leong-Lopes

This is Exactly What I Signed up for

Curled up on the shower floor, I lay imprisoned. Betrayed. Helpless. There was no way out of this system. If I am not fulfilled as a physical therapist, I couldn't imagine how anything would be fulfilling. A dam burst from within me. My vision swirled, then flashed white. And flashed again. The liquid burned as it streamed down my cheeks, hotter than the shower water on my skin.

My face felt like a stress ball that had been squeezed too tight and couldn't rebound back to its neutral state. My very being felt encased, helpless against the cacophony of ringing in my ears, the water drumming against my skull, and defeated thoughts echoing against the shower glass. I crumpled to the slick floor, unable to find anything sturdy enough to grasp onto and ground myself. My shoulders heaved as I gargled through a water-filled breath. I was frozen under the assault of the shower spray just as I was paralyzed in my situation. This is not what I signed up for.

At 14 years of age, I knew in my core that physical therapy was my vocation. I was made to connect with people and serve them. I had both the passion and the skill to bring clarity to the questions people brought to me. It was as true as the sun rising from the east.

Doors kept opening for me as I pursued the profession. I got through high school, college, grad school, and licensure in nine years, with accolades that validated I was going in the right direction. I had a clear path to my desired job and was preparing to take ownership of a clinic.

However, I was unaware that it would take more from me than I was already overexerting myself to give. I was not in line to fulfill my passion. I soon realized that the healthcare system is lacking for our patients as well as for the providers. Naively, I had thought the system would spare no expense to take care of those seeking help and those offering help. I was proven wrong. Not even a year into my working career, I was experiencing burnout.

I now had little hope that I could make a difference in the greater healthcare system to support my aging, pickleball devoted patients from their injuries and meet their desired physical goals. I could assess and treat them, but I was limited in providing them with a safe return to their fulfilling hobbies and activities with preventative medicine. Insurance doesn't cover the whole picture, causing many clinics not to provide that kind of care. Further, my focus is more or less specific to pickleball. A few days after my shower breakdown, I was playing pickleball with my parents. They had gotten into the sport a few years prior and their brightly burning passion for the game quickly caught fire to my inner athlete.

While playing, the despair from a few nights ago eluded me; it had no place when I was on the courts. I focused on the satisfying pop of the ball when it made contact with my paddle, the addicting rush when my shot blew past my opponent, and the wave of relief when I got my paddle out right on time to deflect a volley back over the net, and the stirring sense of accomplishment when my dink was just out of my opponent's reach. It would be so much more fulfilling once I had better power and precision and consistency to direct my shots. I realized how much more fulfilling it would be when I had trained my reflexes and responses to take on any bang, dink or lob, knowing that my best was enough to keep up and make a difference. I wondered how much more I could push my body to change up the game.

Pickleball was easy to pick up, but deceptively demanding on the body. Both in my clinic and at the courts I began seeing a knee brace here, an elbow sleeve there, a guarded bend over to pick up the ball, pitching steps to start and stop a change in direction and wrist fractures. My parents weren't immune to these injuries either, and my chest tightened every time I learned of a new incident. From a PT perspective, of course I wanted them to be conditioned properly for this hobby-turned-lifestyle to stave off injuries and recovery. But as their daughter, I wanted them to be safe, healthy, and well to enjoy their years ahead, sans the acute injuries and chronic pains.

I was thrilled that pickleball was an encompassing package for all aspects of health, enjoyment, and connecting to a community, but lately, I was growing more and more anxious that the next injury was going to be something that left them feeling as helpless as I felt in my career—without a solution that didn't include giving up what they loved.

One month later, I found myself on a strategy call with a healthcare-specific business coach, Greg Todd, who also came from a physical therapist background. He had come across my social media feeds multiple times proclaiming to, "offer solutions and value in the ever-changing world, creating wealth and fulfillment in all aspects of your life." He told me that there are ways to make healthcare accessible to the extent I dream of and that I could serve people the way I want my parents to be served, no longer worrying about burnout or a broken system. I could enjoy what I do to the extent that I may never want to retire, because I was doing what tended to my soul.

Greg asked me what group of people I felt most compelled to serve, and I readily answered, "older adult pickleball athletes." Physicians were reporting an increase in patients presenting with pickleball-related injuries, especially in the older adult population. Information and resources were out there for full injury recovery, return to sport, performance optimization and injury prevention, but it wasn't getting to the players. My current pickleball-devoted patients were getting some training and education from me already, but I wanted to offer it limitlessly to the community beyond the clinic walls as well. The health and wellness world needs to be more accessible to pickleball athletes so they could stay on the courts for years to come.

The swell rising up in me reproduced the tears from the month before, but this time, it signaled a glimmer of hope. Greg had a solution to my problem, and it didn't mean I would have to stop doing physical therapy.

Gratefully, today I am not only still providing physical therapy services, I have specialized in pickleball athletes, offering solutions that enable others to stay on the courts instead of giving up what they love. I get to spend my time talking about and playing a sport I love with people I love meeting. I get to answer recovery and performance questions right there on the courts in real-time. I get to go online and share fun, informative videos and engaging, educational presentations with the greater pickleball community.

The fulfillment from putting away a shot I had intentionally set up, is as joyful as when my clients' eyes light up, finally making sense of their pain and believing in their capacity to get back to playing their hearts out. When I realized there was a solution to my problem, and it didn't mean giving up what I love—that changed everything for me. Not only am I an actual player in this game, I can drastically make a difference.

That desolate woman on the shower floor was now extending her fearless love for her passion into the expanse. Having the self-efficacy and knowledge that we are an active player in our journey is an empowering position. We all want to stay in the "game." We all want to know we can change the game. The feasibility of limitless dreams —that's what I strive to imbue in those who want to get out of pain, get back on the courts, and change the game.

Princess Leong

An Unlikely Singles Run

"Time-out!" I called out to the referee. I signaled with my downward opened palm on top of my paddle as I looked to her to acknowledge my request. "Time out is called by the receiver!" The referee announced. "The score is 14-9. You have one minute." I tried not to limp to the sideline, but my left hamstring was tightening up again. It had been a thorn in my side since the first game of the bronze medal match earlier that evening. I used all my timeouts in that match, whether I was down or ahead on the score, dropping to the ground and using the 45 seconds I had to stretch until I heard the referee wail, "15 seconds!"

I had never planned on playing singles. I felt it was too much running and my small 5'2" frame couldn't possibly cover all that court. Previously, my husband, Mike signed me up for singles at Western Regionals where I won gold. I discovered that I enjoyed singles, and the fact that all responsibility for all hits, strategy, and the mental and emotional fortitude was on me. I was excited to cash in on my golden ticket at Nationals to play more singles.

My start time was at 1pm that afternoon, and now it was rounding 7pm as the court lights started flickering on above the ongoing battles below. The scorching desert heat was gently fading into a pleasant coolness that I shrugged off my cooling scarf that I had worn all day. This was Indian Wells. This was Nationals. Earlier in the day, I got knocked down to the "opportunity bracket" on my second match. Despite my nagging hamstring issue, I slogged through the loser's bracket, fighting to win to stay in the competition. I wanted to fulfill my tournament goal of "winning means you can play more pickleball."

When I got into the bronze medal match, I knew that, even if I lost, I'd still walk away with my first Nationals medal. "Bronze is pretty good at Nationals," I thought. But, when my opponent started falling short to my play, I realized that I could do better than bronze today and that my goal was meager. So, I remained focused, and I won. So, here I was, in the gold medal match. I lost the first game. The score was close. That was encouraging. But I was tired and encumbered by this hamstring. Looking across the net at my opponent, I realized that she, too, was tired. I fought and took the second and third games of that match. Since I made it through the back draw, I was obliged to play the fourth game tie-breaker, a game to 15 points.

Mike was there at the sideline with my water bottle. "You ok?" he asked with concern in his voice. I was on the ground again, stretching and sipping water. My mind was on that score. She was a point away from winning the whole shebang. The point deficit loomed large in my head and, considering my physical state, I didn't think I had a chance, nor the strength to fight any longer. Then, a silly thought ran through my head, which escaped out of my mouth in answer to Mike's inquiry. "I just want to make it to 10 points," I breathed. Reason being, that in the annals of history, people would look at the results of this match and see that my losing score was in the double digits. I felt that it would be a respectable loss. "Just get to 10," I repeated as I got up in answer to the referee's call. "Time in! The score is 14-9!

The singsong voice of the referee seemingly underlined my single-digit score. I slowly sucked in a deep breath, breathing out my whispered mantra before every serve, "Just hit it where she's not." Her serve was lofty and short, inviting me to jog to midcourt and rip my left-handed forehand off the high bounce down the line to her backhand. This sent her hitting on the run. The ball sailed right to me at the net for a soft putaway down the opposite sideline. "Sideout! 9-14!" I had the serve.

"Serve deep," my inner voice sounded instructional, and I obeyed. Surprisingly, her return came back at me with such speed and height. I let it bounce. "OUT!" I exclaimed. "Point! 10-14!" Well then. I had reached my goal for the night. My body was ready to walk off the court right then, but I still had the serve. I might as well go all out and serve big. What did I have to lose? "Dear God," I prayed (for real), "The rest is up to You. Just give me the strength to finish this." She hit another return long. 11-14. My heart started to flutter. The following points were a blur.

My heart was in my mouth the whole time, and my focus turned to keeping my head on and not freaking out. "14-14!" I had the serve. I had to win by two.

The audience had grown in the stands for this battle. Cheering for both me and my opponent got louder and I started to hear individual voices call out my name. Hearing them cemented my determination to finish this. I was exhausted. My legs were jelly. I felt like I was wading through molasses each time I picked up my feet to move. My heart and mind were the only parts of my physical being that were racing. I served. She returned. I hit. She returned. I hit. She returned ... into the net. "15-14!" My heart was going to explode. It seemed to have reached its limit from the physical effort and adrenaline. My body kept telling me, "You did good! Take it easy now, and let her win. Silver for your first Nationals is outstanding."

My mind wouldn't give up. It kept willing me to stay upright and it commandeered my body to do its will and not squander this opportunity to finish well. One more mantra spoken. I served more cautiously this time. Her return was deep to my forehand and I blipped the ball cross-court, short, to her backhand. She scrambled forward and barely got to the ball. I saw her predicament and closed in on the net just as she waffled it over at my feet as I was running up. I was jammed. All I could do was chip it straight ahead. Out of the corner of my eye I saw her already moving to the center of her court. She was going to get to it! Like a silent movie in slow motion, I saw her belabored steps to the ball ... her outstretched arm ... her desperate swing ... the miss. The roar of the crowd jolted me into the reality of the moment. I did it. I was a Nationals singles champion! I've imagined a moment like this ... both my hands raised overhead, waving and thanking the cheering crowd, my heart full of elation and pride. But it played out so differently that night. My first feeling was empathy for my opponent's loss.

For the past hour, my eyes had been focused on the woman across the net, and as that ball sailed past her, my eyes watched her head bowed down and her shoulders slump in defeat. "That could've been me,", I thought. I flung my arms open wide and beckoned her to me. She stumbled to me and we wearily embraced, the net pinned between us, our parched, cackling voices exclaiming our appreciation for each other's play.

As we turned to walk down the net to thank the referee, and for me to sign the scorecard, it was then that the feelings of elation and celebration came flooding over me. The next morning, I reflected on the day on my social media: "I am truly humbled. I learned so much about the human spirit when drawing strength from God yesterday. It was a grueling 6 hours in the desert heat, playing out full matches of three games, and a four-game gold medal match.

I learned not to settle for less, because when you have God-given capabilities and opportunities, you should never be lazy. Yes, I secretly was aiming for bronze, but when openings came in the bronze medal match, I chose to dig in. Even in the gold medal 15-point tiebreaker, when I was losing with my opponent at 14 and me at 9, I just wanted to get to 10 so the brackets would look respectable. Again, settling for less. But, I'm glad I listened to God and my human spirit to just get one more point and another. Hang in there though my legs are cramping and my breath is burning in my lungs."

Lesson learned: don't settle for less when you really do have what it takes, because a Nationals Gold is amazing!

Laurie Loney

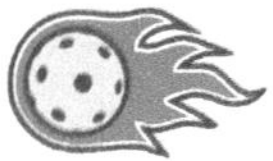

Pukaball, an Hawaiian Playground

I am a pickleball teacher, player, matchmaker, rule checker, partner finder, fan, friend and therapist. I am a champion for all levels and all players. In Hawaii we call it Pukaball. Puka means "hole" in Hawaiian. I'm not really sure why that name stuck, but it did. My father coined it Pukaball in the late 60s after meeting the game's originators from Bainbridge Island, Washington. They were on vacation in Maui enjoying the beach when they introduced my neighbors and my family to this wonderful game. It wasn't long after that Dad built us our own, patchwork surface court—the first pickleball court in all of the Hawaiian isles. We didn't have discretionary funds to spend on a fancy court, but to me, our funky court was just perfect.

Now in my sixties, I've been playing "Pukaball" for more than 50 years. We have introduced this sport to numerous friends and acquaintances over the years, hosting parties and other fun gatherings. I feel as though I've been an ambassador of sorts since the beginning. I've actually lost count of how many friends I've introduced to the game. It makes me happy to know how much they love pickleball now.

By 2015 pickleball had grown, including professional players and tournaments were now being held. My childhood neighbor Megan and I were excited to enter our first official tournament (the Aloha State Senior Games) that same summer in Kona. By the end Megan was feeling like a zombie and my back went out. However, we managed to survive being out of shape, the extreme heat, and four grueling championship games to win a gold medal. Talk about joy! I happily crossed that item off my bucket list.

Not long after I was laid off from my job of nearly 20 years. I was unemployed, stressed out, and trying to find a new job. I admit I was feeling pretty low and a bit lost. I was starting to panic. What job could I possibly do now? After some weeks of searching, it occurred to me that I could turn our home court (built in 2003) into a small business. I decided I would give lessons as I had done numerous times before. I also realized that the visitors to our beautiful island were desperately looking for somewhere to play pickleball. The game was just catching on here and very few courts existed on Maui. My husband, "Pocket" and I worked hard to improve the old court and the surrounding pathetic landscaping.

I soon created my website pickleballmaui.com and a social media page with the same name. I got my first customers that December. I was very nervous, but also very excited. I put out flowers and made leis for them. A visitor wanted to surprise her husband with a Maui pickleball experience for his birthday. I was thrilled to help her make that happen. It was a big hit. People were searching for local, unique activities that are outside of the normal tourist activities. Pickleball at my house would fit the bill—a unique experience far from the glam resorts. More and more tourists began coming to my court. They enjoyed playing with locals, in a beautiful, fenceless setting, surrounded by avocado and macadamia nut trees. They loved hearing of my history with the sport too, and it wasn't long before I started selling "Maui Pukaball" shirts and hats. Business started out slow, however, with each booking I was elated. My dream job was coming true. I was meeting people from all over the world with the same love for pickleball. My customers were mostly tourists, and occasionally locals taking lessons and setting up matches. In the beginning it was a sweet, part-time job that made me incredibly happy.

By 2016 I became an ambassador for the USA Pickleball Association. Along with a few other ambassadors, we worked to promote pickleball across the island by teaching the game and lobbying with the county for more courts. Public courts have been slowly added to tennis courts, however we have a long way to go. In 2018 Jennifer Lucore, a pickleball pro and national champion, and her mother Beverly Youngren, contacted me about writing a chapter in their book ***The History of Pickleball***. My chapter is called "Pukaball - Early Years on Maui." I was honored to have my beautiful court also featured in the USA Pickleball official magazine as well as in **Central Oregon Pickleball magazine**.

Business at Pickleball Maui grew slowly and steadily until COVID hit our island. In March 2020 Maui was put in lockdown and the public gyms and outdoor courts were closed. I decided to offer low COVID rates for locals to rent my court or to take socially distanced lessons. Suddenly everyone wanted to learn how to play. Pickleball was spreading so fast it was hard to believe. Soon my little part-time business was booming and at near capacity.

I always dreamed of having my own business, but I never imagined it would come to include the game I have loved all my life. I feel this is my destiny and now people call me the "Pukaball Queen of Maui." I get tremendous joy in meeting people, teaching new players, creating new friendships, helping people get fit, and hearing the laughter and happy screams on my court all day long. How lucky am I? Pickleball is so much more than a sport. It's a rebirth for seniors — bringing them back into a fun, physical activity, which they desperately crave. It is awesome to watch the new friendships evolve from this game, and I love seeing young athletes realize that pickleball is not only crazy fun for seniors, it's also a challenging workout for youth.

Pickleball has empowered me to introduce this amazing game to all manner of people, and to watch them grow and blossom. This sport literally changes people's lives for the better. I've seen the miraculous transformation that can take place. I have seen lonely new Maui residents suddenly have a multitude of dear friends. I have seen love connections blossom from playing this game. I have seen heavy people lose weight and get fit. I have seen 10-year-olds having a blast with 70-year-olds. I have seen different ethnic groups getting to know each other. I have seen people working together to get and maintain more public courts, giving up their time for tournaments, hosting charity pickleball events, and giving equipment to school kids. The list goes on and on! It seems to bring out the Aloha Spirit in people.

I hear it's not really a job if you love what you do. For me, that is so true. Pickleball was a gift given to me, that I in turn, am privileged to pass on to so many people. It warms my heart and makes me feel important. I have the backs of all my pickleball friends and students, and they have mine. I am pickleball and pickleball defines me.

Cindy Lutz

Ambassadors of Pickleball

I'm a bulldog when it comes to getting pickleball courts built at local city parks. It started with a cement slab in our backyard—leftover from a sports court back in 1985. After discovering pickleball, I realized this could be our very own home court. My husband Bob painted the court and purchased a net. We lived far from town. I figured no one would want to drive out to my house to play. However, on my 60th birthday I had a party and invited all my friends including my pickleball friends. When they arrived they said why didn't I tell them I had a court. I now understand the saying "Build it and they will come."

I had never heard of pickleball until around 2012. After I participated in a badminton senior Olympic tournament, a few people mentioned another sport called pickleball. It intrigued me, so I found out where it was played (two indoor recreation centers) . I checked it out and was hooked.

A year later my husband started playing. He's always been athletic and great with coaching abilities. We started inviting my indoor recreation player friends over for Sunday morning play as we were just beginning to hear about pickleball tournaments. At that time tournaments were all held outdoors. I wanted my indoor group to come over to play so that they could get some experience playing outdoor pickleball. Soon I had close to twelve regular Sunday morning players in the group. I put out coffee and soon others were bringing snacks. We would play from 7:30am til 11:30am.

One day I was at a neighbor's yard sale and they asked if I was holding Sunday services at my house. I relayed that story to my Sunday play group and one Sunday, everyone came to play with their Sunday church-going attitude. We had Sister Margaret (all dressed up as a nun) had Bibles, rosary in hands, and Pastor Bob (aka my husband) led the group in the religious experience of playing pickleball with good intentions. Sister Margaret also wrote up the ten commandments of pickleball. We had a great time. Around 2015 my friend from Goodyear, AZ who is a Pickleball Ambassador, mentioned that I should also become a USA Pickleball Ambassador. Not thinking too seriously about that proposal I said maybe Bob can be one. She submitted our names and we became co-USA Pickleball Ambassadors.

After a few years of hosting play at my house I was hearing lots of pickleball news about outdoor courts being built further north of Tucson. I was bummed that no one was talking about building pickleball courts here in Tucson so I emailed the Tucson mayor asking why we do not have any outdoor courts. The Major referred me to the City Parks Director and I made an appointment. I gathered three other local USA Pickleball Ambassadors and another gal that had some courts built at her association and she guided us on how to approach the city about courts.

That first meeting didn't go well as she quickly told us that the City of Tucson Parks had no money. Our small group of five decided that we needed more players and created a local pickleball club called Tucson Area Pickleball Club (TAP). We submitted paperwork on behalf of our club and became a 501(c)(4) organization created to promote the development of the sport of pickleball for the recreation and health of residents in the greater Tucson area. As a club we collaborated with the city and provided monies to the Tucson Parks Foundation for pickleball-related items. Bob and I were founding members and I was elected president of the club, which I did for five years. After many City of Tucson Board meetings and having our TAP club members attend we finally got the okay to have twelve outdoor dedicated pickleball courts. We had a ribbon-cutting event at the UDALL pickleball courts which has become the go-to place to play in Tucson.

Pickleball was going great and my husband and I were fully into playing this wonderful game when in 2016 he had a stroke. In his mid-50s he had suffered a heart attack. But the stroke was so much more debilitating than his heart attack. After seeing him in the hospital unable to get in and out of bed I thought that this condition was going to be life-changing for the both of us. His left side and his speech was affected and he had to learn to walk again.

Little did we know that the game of pickleball was going to be a lifesaver for my husband and me. When the stroke happened and he was doing therapy to walk again, he let the nursing staff know that he had to get back to playing pickleball. Once he explained to them the game of pickleball they brought in foam paddles and foam balls to get him back into playing the game he loved so much. Slowly the nursing staff had him moving and getting his hand-eye coordination going using the form paddles and ball. Once home, we had nurses, a speech therapist and a physical therapist came to the house and slowly his mobility came back.

Our Sunday group gave back to us more than they know. They were such an inspiration to him and I am so thankful for their patience and kindness during his days of healing. This group continued to come to the house to play and always included Bob on the court. He started playing in his wheelchair, then a walker and then a cane. Before we knew it he was back playing. His balance is still a bit off and his stamina probably isn't what it used to be, however, anyone who has just met him would never imagine that he had a stroke.

We now have a family business called Lutz Pickleball Academy that my son, Todd started.. This gives us an opportunity to show other people how to play this fun sport. Pickleball truly is a game anyone can play regardless of their sport experience or lack of. It's a great social game and I'm happy that I help connect people to other players and places to play in Tucson.

Some of the pickleball-related things we were able to do over the years include; Our Facebook Page -Tucson Pickleball Buddies with 1.4K members, giving lessons to kids at recreation centers, demonstrating the game to Southern Arizona PE teachers and being founding members of Tucson Arizona Pickleball Club (TAP).

I am still aggressively always looking for pickleball court opportunities as there are many unused tennis courts at many parks around town that could be converted. Currently there are two parks that will soon have additional dedicated pickleball courts opening up hopefully this year.

Pickleball has been not only a great connection for our family, but it has also given new life to us. I'm ever so thankful that I found pickleball, I got my husband hooked and we continue our love of the game to this day.

Kelli McRobert

Good Sports

The sweat runs down my face, and stings my eyes, yet I am focused, balanced and calm as the world around me has suddenly gone quiet. A crowd has gathered, inquisitive, curious as to how this game can still be playing out. 45 minutes of play has brought us to this moment. Best two out of three, no cap, and we have suddenly regained the serve. But I have jumped ahead a few years, so let me take you back to the beginning.

My mother had recently passed away and I was struggling with grief and persistent sadness. I felt that I needed to establish some type of goal to regain my focus and motivation. I set a plan in motion to complete 50 road races by the time I was 50.

Fast forward a couple of years and I had already completed over 100 races that included triathlons, marathons, half marathons and anything that had a finish line and was over 5K. Every season, including snowshoe racing, I was out there battling the elements along with my inner demons, still struggling with the loss even after years of competing. The goals continued to become more challenging, like not repeating the same race twice, winter races, and World Championships, then it all came crashing down on me.

In August 2016, I completed two races in 47-degree heat, when I suffered a "heart incident" (SVT) and was transported by ambulance to the cardiac unit at Milton General. This was my wake-up call, to reconsider my choice of sport, and accept that I was over 50 and that I may want to find a different hobby as the heart specialist suggested, as I may not get a second chance if this were to happen again.

I headed back to the yoga studio, walked extensively and yet still felt like something was missing, that competitive rush, that feeling of belonging to a group and planning fun weekends away for events. It just so happened I met someone who mentioned the word pickleball during a yoga coloring session and I was intrigued. We chatted a bit more and it was decided I would come out to the YMCA and give it a try with another gal pal.

We were hooked. Paddles ordered and balls in hand, we were ready to go. I joined a local group and jumped in with both feet. I was on all the committees and boards and began to learn all the ins and outs of the game, strategies and how to improve my play through online videos and private coaching sessions.

Within a few years, I had improved enough to play at a competitive level and was proudly standing on podiums for both doubles and mixed events. We often joked that our husbands were pickleball widows as we joined the tournament circuit and went from town to town spending weekends away, playing, eating and waiting courtside for our next match to be called.

As with any sport there are the highs and lows that come with competitive play. I had many moments throughout my journey where I had to walk away in frustration or take a different approach to a devastating loss that had brought me to tears.

I was both physically and mentally exhausted from a battle hard fought. Is it more difficult to place 4th, missing the podium, or to come in 3rd when a gold or silver was just a few points away? Quite honestly, therapy has helped me work through some of my issues directly connected to competitive sports. A parallel to my deepest emotions, human interactions, disappointments, conflicts, wins and everyday losses. Does it make it any easier? No. I still play to win. However, as I continue to learn and grow in the sport, I am learning to navigate both the highs and lows.

Over the next few years, I continued to actively work with various organizations like Pickleball Canada and Pickleball Ontario, realizing that I really enjoyed welcoming new players to the sport, meeting new friends and sharing a common interest in everything pickleball. I found the more I learned, the more I wanted to learn. It was a renewed focus as I waded into the world of becoming a certified level 2 referee.

I felt empowered as I better understood the rules that governed this inclusive sport. I worked hard to improve my skills and teaching abilities while earning my National Coaching Certification Levels 1 & 2 and completing my Professional Pickleball Registry credential. They say knowledge is power. For me, it was a way to truly understand the sport from the inside out.

As I had never really played a racquet sport, a lot of the key concepts were foreign to me. Seeing, trying and applying a skill helped me to understand the whys, when, and hows. And this, in turn, helped me more aptly present the information to new players.

My passion was playing, and I began to advocate for new courts in our area, as our current selection of places to play was slim to none. Each year, I would choose another area to promote and build grassroots momentum so we could demonstrate the growth of the sport and begin to build and repurpose outdoor courts hoping that indoor locations would soon follow. While the politics of recreational complexes is outside of my realm, I enjoyed presenting to council and seeking out support for the various local projects as they continued to evolve. I met other like minded folk who were champions of the sport and would advocate at every opportunity to support the sport locally.

As with any sport, winning is always a ton of fun. A proud moment as you get your photo taken, sweaty and red faced for many of us, after a day of competitive play. Proudly displaying your achievements on Facebook for all to see. However, it is not always the win that is first and foremost in many of these events. Sitting courtside is an opportunity to meet someone new. Find out a bit about them, ask questions and if you are lucky forge a friendship that extends beyond the pickleball court.

As I mentioned, one of the most memorable games for me was our gold medal match at the Provincials being held in Ottawa. The heat was unbearable, and I was having flashbacks to the day on the mountainside as I struggled to finish, nauseous and longing for a cold drink and some A/C. I could feel the fear welling up inside as I hoped I was not repeating my 'heart incident' yet again.

We were in our final game and had been playing for more than 45 minutes. The crowd was cheering on every point, every shot and rooting for either of us to win. The play itself was epic, drives perfectly redirected and partners working as one. Cross court dinking that was low and aggressive with planned plays to draw our opponents apart or set us up for the perfect shot.

19-19 and we manage to regain the serve. Our timeouts are spent. We are running on adrenaline at this point and the spectators are motivating the play.

We serve, they return and the fire fight begins, slowed down slightly by the perfect reset, waiting, waiting, for that opportune moment for us to attack. Our opponent pops the ball up as my partner attacks. I lay in wait for a returned ball but it's hit in to the net. Score now 20-19. Pressure is on. We take our time, paddle tap, and get in position, ready for what we hope is the final serve, a gold medal on the line. Both teams started to show a few cracks, exhausted, sweaty, and yet, still positive, fair and friendly.

The next rally seems to go on forever and the crowd has surrounded our court adding oohs and ahs at each drive, volley and dink. Into the net it goes. Second serve, 20-19-2. The final rally is a blur. I feel as though all I can see and hear is the ball, in slow motion as it goes back and forth a number of times, each team just trying to keep it in play, nobody wanting to be the one to make the error.

A few more dinks and then a quick switch up, as the opponent has briefly dropped their paddle, caught up in the excitement of her partner's game. Thud, the ball strikes her in the chest and the game is over, 21-19. Gold medal for us. EPIC. But the story does not end here, as we approached the net, everyone in tears, it was an instant in time that will forever be in my heart.

At that moment, as we were completely drained, physically and emotionally, we made a pure connection, a bond of sorts, as we had shared this memorable game. We played hard, but we played fair and complimented each other after each well placed shot.

The true meaning of sportsmanship was apparent and friendships were founded that continue to this day. For me, pickleball is a way to stay active, as I continue to navigate the aging process, while maintaining a social connection with others. Friendship, fun, and a renewed focus on living life to the fullest, one great game at a time.

Petra Michael

A Transformative Journey

When the world was hit by the COVID-19 pandemic, my husband Shawn and I knew that we had to make some crucial changes to our daily routines. Travel was severely restricted, leaving many of us with few options for entertainment. Days blurred together as work consumed our lives. Shawn was an avid pick-up basketball player, but the risk of contracting the virus and spreading it to our family was too great. Thus, we decided that he should find a safer physical activity, one that would minimize the risk of transmission.

Shawn's search led him back to the Bobby Riggs Tennis Club in Encinitas, California. He was eager to re-ignite his love for tennis, having won the Seattle City Tennis Championship at the age of 10 & played in leagues when he had moved to Southern California around 2000. But what really caught our attention was the transformation of the tennis courts into Pickleball courts, with the pickleball players sporting athletic clothing for tennis, yoga and soccer.

As an experienced fashion designer from Europe, I realized that there was a gap in the market for Pickleball-specific activewear that was unique and fashion-forward. We began playing at Poinsettia Park in Carlsbad and the Bobby Riggs Tennis Club. As I played, it was clear that pickleball was not just a fun game but also a great way to stay active and cope with the stress and uncertainty of the pandemic. Playing pick-up games with others in the park, I felt the joy and camaraderie that the sport brought to my life.

I'm originally from Germany. I was a graduate of fashion design in Rome, Italy and I've worked as a corporate hospitality sales professional, based in the United States. With our shared passion for fashion and sports, Shawn and I took on the challenge of developing two pickleball paddles that have since been approved by the USAPA, as well as a European inspired color forward line of Pickleball activewear for men and women. Our journey has been nothing short of thrilling and we are proud to be contributing to the growth of pickleball while promoting safe physical activity during the pandemic.

It all started with a dramatic turn of events that led us down an unexpected path of creativity and innovation. As I reflect on my journey, I realize how much pickleball has transformed my life. It was not just a sport that I picked up to stay active during the pandemic, but it was an experience that brought about a significant change in my physical and mental health. Before discovering pickleball, I was stuck in a high-pressure corporate sales job that kept me tied to a desk and traveling across the United States. I was always sedentary, and hardly had any time for myself. As I delved deeper into the world of pickleball, I marveled at the transformative impact this sport has had on my physical health and wellbeing. My endurance, agility and overall fitness gained significant improvements and my daily step count skyrocketed from just 500 to over

10,000 thanks to the fast paced nature of the game. But pickleball's effects didn't stop at just my physical health—it also improved my hand-eye coordination, balance and flexibility.

With the encouragement and support of my husband and pickleball partner, I left my corporate job and dedicated myself to developing a line of activewear, from concept to production. The journey was challenging, but it was also incredibly rewarding. We spent countless hours designing, sourcing materials and evaluating the activewear line and paddles. Finally, after months of hard work, we launched the SKYblue Pickleball brand and continue to develop our company.

Initially, pickleball provided a much needed escape from the stress and uncertainty of the pandemic. Playing with others in the park brought joy and camaraderie to my life, and I found myself feeling more energized and focused both on and off the court. Pickleball provided a mental health booster that has transformed my mood and outlook on life. The combination of fun and social interactions that have come with playing pickleball have provided an outlet for stress relief that is akin to a therapy session but with a paddle in my hand. The game demands my focus and concentration which clears my mind and frees me from daily stressors. As I move and groove on the court, the physical activity releases endorphins that bring joy and eases anxiety.

It was a beautiful spring day when I met Toni at the park while playing. We found ourselves playing against two men. As the game progressed, it became apparent that this was turning into a classic "battle of the sexes." The male opponents began to show resentment towards us but Toni and I refused to be intimidated. We fought back and emerged victorious. Despite our win, Toni and I felt that playing like that took away some of the fun of the game. Toni must have sensed my unease, because she then invited me to join a group of ladies who played at two private pickleball courts. At first, I was hesitant and a bit nervous. But as I started to play with these women, I found myself enjoying the game even more. I formed new relationships with the ladies in the group on and off the court, and the bond we formed is unbreakable. Playing pickleball with my friends is not just about staying active and healthy, it is also an opportunity to catch up and socialize. We always take a break in the mid-afternoon to enjoy a potluck lunch together, chatting and laughing as we refuel. Missing a Sunday pickleball session is simply not an option for us. We value the time we spend together too much, and the bond we have formed through our shared love of the game is very strong.

When I traveled to Europe recently, as I boarded the plane, I knew that my passion for pickleball would follow me across the ocean. With several SKYblue Pickleball paddles in my luggage, I set out on a mission to share the love for the game with as many people as possible. Upon arriving, I wasted no time and contacted the local city officials to learn where I could play pickleball. They referred me to the TBC Sports Club, and to my delight, the club was excited to meet me and learn more about the game. However, since it was summertime, we had to wait until fall to meet in person.

Undeterred, I called up some old high-school friends and shared my love for pickleball. Eva, who teaches at a local school, offered the large outdoor space on the schoolyard to create our very own pickleball court. With the help of some chalk and an old badminton net, we designed the court and got to playing.

My friends learned the rules quickly, including the fact that the "kitchen" was a non-volley zone. Our game even attracted the attention of a passersby, who stopped to watch us play. By the end of the day, my high school friends were hooked and eager to play again. The next day, we expanded our group by inviting friends of friends to join in on the fun. We turned it into a pickleball and pizza party, which got more competitive and enjoyable as the night wore on. When it was time for me to leave, I left my paddles and balls with my friends. As I boarded the plane back home, I knew that the love for pickleball would continue to spread and bring joy to others.

Through the simple act of playing a game, I was able to connect with old friends, make new ones, and inspire others to try out a new sport and enjoy the simple pleasures in life. Pickleball has been a transformative experience that has brought about a significant change in my life. It has given me the inspiration to pursue my passion and create something of which I am truly proud. I am grateful for this journey and excited to see what the future holds.

Janice Mundee 

Love at First Sight

I met Ted through music more than a decade ago. Together we started a band where he plays guitar and I sing. At the time, I would exercise, go to the gym and attend the occasional class, nothing too strenuous. Then one day, I heard about this new sport and thought I'd give it a try. It was love at first sight—just like meeting Ted! I literally went from minimal activity to playing pickleball, sometimes in 105 degree weather, for three hours or more. I attribute this huge shift in my life to the passion that comes with the game.

I am usually up for the "one more game" despite being 100% drained. I sometimes play every day and sometimes even two times a day. As my intensity and focus has grown, I have taken classes, clinics, trained and entered tournament competition. In 2021 I won a gold medal at the USAPA Nationals! For many competitive players, Nationals is the big year-end goal. The tournament is difficult to get into and very competitive once you're there.

Due to the increase and intensity of activity, I have become much stronger with greater endurance. I've also had to learn how to be an athlete: recover from injuries, warm up, stretch, condition and eat properly. Aside from all the physical advantages, the other incredible bonus is that I have had the good fortune through pickleball to meet so many people, not only in my hometown, but across the United States. We share this love and passion for the game.

I am convinced that as a species we are meant to have our tribe. We are meant to have connections and a feeling of belonging. Pickleball gives this to us and is one of the foundations of the sport's popularity and addictiveness. At one of my first tournaments, after traveling 300 miles and staying two nights in a hotel and paying for entry fees, food and lodging, the final cost was roughly $1,000. I looked around at all of the great people, and thought, I should find people to stay with, and I could then offer them lodging if they come to my area. Thus began my venture into a new business called Picklebilly: hosted housing for pickleball players world-wide.

After many iterations, Picklebilly has a Facebook group as well as a web page. People can join for free to be hosts, guests, or both. We have hosts in Australia, Canada, and throughout the United States. Members set up their own travel arrangements using picklebilly.com. I have met terrific people who have come and stayed with my husband Ted and me. I've also traveled, stayed in lovely homes, and made new pickleball friends who love the sport just like I do. What started as a way to save money, has evolved to something even more important: promoting human connectivity. I am always inspired by seeing players connecting through my site. It makes me happy to realize that I found a need and am filling it through Picklebilly.

I also helped launch The Pickleball Workbook journal/planner for the improving player. And to further delve into the world of pickleball, I became a certified instructor and have held numerous clinics for new players. Watching someone discover this sport is very uplifting.

To say pickleball has changed me is an understatement. Pickleball is changing the world. In our divided country, pickleball brings people together, regardless of age, race, gender, sexual orientation, religion or politics. When you are playing, none of those things are important. What's important is knowing whether you are server one or server two and the score. I see a bright and positive future for this sport and its influence on our communities. I know it has brought much joy and goodness to my life.

Mo Nard

I Got Off the Couch

I was born into a tennis playing family. I played from the age of four. I also played every sport I could get my hands on—swimming, volleyball, discus throwing, sprints and hurdles, basketball, snow skiing and cycling. In my freshman year of high school I was invited to play racquetball with a friend who had been playing awhile. I beat her. A passion was born. I wound up winning two national championship titles in women's 19 and under doubles (1982 and 1983), along with many other titles.I became a successful racquetball teaching pro and taught as far away as Nagoya, Japan.

By 1985 I had become completely burned out on racquetball and competition in general. I joined the US Air Force and began my 35 year long career as an x-ray technologist. On September 11, 1986, I was in a military exercise at my new duty station, Elmendorf Air Force Base, Alaska. I was freezing cold and participating in a lifting class, when I lifted one of my fellow airmen and suffered a life changing back injury. I have hurt every day since then. I learned of my mortality that day. I had once been a fearless person and then I became much more fearful of injury in everything I did.

After my four year commitment was up, I came back home to Sacramento, California and returned to civilian life. I still played racquetball here and there and did a bit of cycling, but for the most part, I was a couch potato. At age 38 I was noticing that after I would play racquetball, I would limp pretty badly the next day due to hip pain. At 39, I finally saw a doctor. A few doctors later, I was diagnosed with bilateral congenital hip dysplasia. My hip sockets are too shallow to properly hold the ball part of my hip joints. I had been born with a condition that wasn't diagnosed for all of those years. I thought everyone's hips hurt on long car rides or that everyone had to kind of pop their hip to get out of the car sometimes.

I was only 39 but I was often using a cane to get around, especially at work. Three days after I turned 40, I had a right Ganz Periacetabular Osteotomy. I had the same surgery on my left side two years later. This is a complex surgery. Each time, the pelvis is broken in three places, muscles are detached and reattached, the hip socket is rotated over the hip in a more favorable position and then some very long screws are put in to hold everything in place. The recovery for these surgeries is long and painful. I have since had all of the hardware removed in two more surgeries and it is all my own bone in there, for now.

The hip surgery years, 2004-2007, did nothing to break me out of my couch potato ways. Once I was fully recovered, I did some hiking, biking and whitewater rafting, but nothing on a daily or even weekly basis. By this time, I had also developed severe depression, which helped adhere me to the couch even more.

In late 2016, my wife told me about a game that her friend had been playing. It was called pickleball. I'd never heard about that sport. She gave me a little beginner's set of wooden paddles and two balls for Christmas. We batted the balls around at my sister's house on Christmas morning and had a blast. A few months later, my sister Lisa told me she'd just taken an introduction to pickleball class at her tennis club and that I should definitely try it. She sent me a YouTube video on scoring and one on rules and then I met her the next day at an indoor facility.

I won my very first game. The game was so easy for me. It felt amazing to have a paddle in my hand. I wanted MORE! It wasn't long before I was fully addicted and competing in tournaments. I met my friend, Reine Steel and we became best buds very quickly. We would gather all of our friends together and teach them how to play. Eventually, someone said, "Why don't you charge money for this?" A business was born. Reine and I formed a company called Positive Dinking™. I soon began to realize that I loved teaching pickleball as much as I loved to play.

Things really took off after that. I became a sponsored player for Head and Penn Pickleball. Then they made me their Regional Marketing Coordinator for Northern California. I became a contributor to the "I Used to Be Somebody" podcast and newsletter by Pickleball Media. My couch was starting to lose the deep butt impression I had forged.

My life opened up again because of pickleball. My identities as an athlete and a coach were reborn. I was getting a steady dose of endorphins. I expanded my social circle by leaps and bounds, meeting some of the nicest people you'd ever want to meet. Pickleball scooped me up and carried me when I needed help. I have the seven very long screws from my surgeries in my pickleball bag to remind me of where I have been, what I have endured and that I should be grateful for the gift of those seven screws, as they gave me many years of increased activity.

Now, my hips are failing again and my back is quite severe, but I know my sport is still there for me. I have retired from play, but I co-authored the book Pickleball for Dummies and I continue to teach lessons and clinics. I will continue to attend tournaments to hang out, coach and cheer for my friends. Most importantly, I will be forever grateful for all that pickleball has given me—identity, community and joy.

Dianne "Snooky" O'Leary 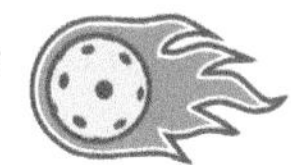

A Reason to Get Up in the Morning

Patrick James O'Leary was my soul mate. We knew from the beginning that we would journey in life together, forever. We met at 17 and 20. I was working at Aerospace where he was a drafter. I was in the document library. We were each other's first boyfriend and girlfriend. A kind-hearted man. I can't even recall an argument in the more than 35 years we were together. We had similar interests and were dedicated parents and grandparents.

So when Patrick suddenly was gone due to a cardiac event, I was lost. My heart turned to dust. The path of grief was profound. I tried to be a strength for the children and grandchildren, but it proved too difficult for me. My belief system carried me through but the days were long and I struggled to get by. Patrick and I were both athletic and had considered playing pickleball, however we never did try playing. A counselor recommended I read a book on grieving. One of the suggestions was to find something new that you didn't do as a couple. This was important so that the activity would be mine and I wouldn't relate it to my loved one.

I could hear the donk donk donk of pickleball nearby in my Simi Valley neighborhood. I skeptically signed up for a parks and rec lesson. I borrowed a paddle and remember walking toward the lesson where everyone was laughing and smiling. I pulled the paddle up close to my chest thinking, "I can't do this." I had the biggest lump in my throat. But I wanted to try. It was so difficult, I was so broken. After the lessons, I started open play with all the older people. They were all so very welcoming.

At first I played during the day and then I added playing at night. I was relatively good at the game, which encouraged me to continue. I didn't go there to make new friends. Honestly, I didn't want any new friendships. Funny, but now I have 100 new friends. The most wonderful people have come into my life from this game. Pickleball helped me forget my problems and distracted me from my grief. It took seven months until I could utter the "f" word: Fun. I was having fun for the first time in such a long time. Pickleball is a big part of my life now. I have friendships that I didn't want or expect.

Acute grief can last up to two years and pickleball has helped bridge the gap. I try to remember that there was a day when I was a beginner. I welcome all levels to the courts and encourage new players to check it out. I have advanced to a 4.0 level and enjoy drilling with friends who like to compete. I try to keep my play at a fun level and haven't played tournaments. Pickleball for me is a place for distraction from life's issues, a place for not feeling the pressure. I prefer not to have to play to win, although I do play to win. As in life, there is pickleball drama. I try to stay out of the drama but it exists—that's just part of it all. The first time I came to play I said I was new and was rejected. I nearly didn't go back. Then I was rejected again. Coach Thomas steered me to higher-level courts and I took a chance and jumped in. That was the starting point.

I encourage people who are athletic to come out and play. If someone is able to move, they would be amazed at how easy it is to learn and how easy it is to make friends. Once someone tries pickleball—get your tent and sleeping bag—cuz you'll never leave the court afterward. Sometimes people don't know that I'm not married since I wear gloves. They ask about my husband. I tell them I'm widowed. They may think I am lonely. But I have 24 nieces and nephews, 25 great nieces and nephews and four grandchildren. Between family and pickleball, my life is full.

Pickleball has improved my life by taking me through my grief journey. Even though I still talk about Patrick a lot, my heart is healed and I am not at all lonely. I am physically out in the sunshine getting exercise, which also helps me stay mentally well. I have a big reason to get up in the morning: pickleball.

Johanna Payne

Just By Chance

I offered to help my good friends Gerrie and Patsy work their booth at the 2021 National Pickleball Tournament in Indian Wells, California. I had never played Pickleball and did not know how to play the game. I decided that since I like to volunteer, I would go ahead and attend an event I knew nothing about. It was important that I got out and experienced life again.

Only three short years ago I was devastated when my loving husband of 34 years passed away. I lost my confidence. I was deeply depressed. My girlfriends kept me going, encouraging me to live life again. I briefly tried the dating scene, but I found it hard to make a connection with anyone. Instead, I just kept myself busy with my girlfriends.

After losing my husband, I began spending my winters in California to be closer to my son and away from the cold in Colorado. I have lived in the mountains of Colorado for more than 50 years, but I'm a Southern girl born in Louisiana with strong family ties in the Baton Rouge/New Orleans area. Many of my Colorado friends spend much of the winter in Palm Springs, California, not far from where my son and granddaughter live—about two hours north of the area.

So when my friends rented a booth at the National Pickleball Tournament, I quickly accepted the invitation. It wasn't too far and I could be of service to them. They were there to sell their children's book, "Pickleball Patsy." They invited me to help them in their booth by bringing lunch, giving them a break, or whatever they needed me to do. Although the tournament was held for an entire week, I originally planned to help with the booth only on the weekend.

What an exciting atmosphere it was to arrive at the beautiful Indian Wells Tennis and Pickleball Center. Margaritaville music was joyfully playing on the loudspeakers, there were festive colorful Adirondack chairs scattered about, and a handful of bars, beer gardens and lots of pickleball booths with free samples and equipment for sale.

On my first day there, they were announcing the winners of the latest game. I was surprised that most of the people attending the event were actually in my age group, 55 and over. They were all dressed in athletic gear, laughing, talking amongst each other and creating a fun atmosphere on a chilly, sunny day. I quickly realized that I loved this type of atmosphere and that I wanted to be included in this pickleball lifestyle. At the booth my girlfriends were meeting lots of interesting people. One of the first ones I was introduced to was Dotti Berry, founder of the website Pickleball Forum For Women and co-author of this book.

Right away Dotti and I were off watching games, meeting her clients and friends, enjoying the event and getting to know each other. She filled me in all about Pickleball. Then she delicately quizzed me about my life details. I told her I was cautiously thinking about finding another partner. That's when Dotti had an idea. She had encouraged her high school friend and pickleball coach from Atlanta, Kenny Beshers, to meet her at the tournament. He was hesitant about going to California, but finally agreed to go at the last minute. She thought it would be a good idea for Kenny and me to meet. She thought we'd be a good match.

We met the following day. Dotti was right, he was a perfect match. We both felt instant love for one another. Kenny is a true Southern gentleman from Atlanta and a great pickleball coach. He is highly respected by all his friends and opponents, and a fun-loving outdoorsy man. We have been together a little more than a year now, having a wonderful time traveling all over Louisiana, Colorado, Atlanta and California. We attended the Nationals in Indian Wells for the second time this year and celebrated our first dating anniversary. We are now gratefully engaged to be married this summer.

We are so happy playing Pickleball, working out and living together at seventy years old. It's our second chance in life and in love. I thank Dotti, Gerrie and Patsy for giving me the life-changing experience through pickleball, a forever gift of friendship.

Carly Penfold

From the Darkness into the Light

There is always a silver lining in difficult situations. I remember the moment of clarity when I came to the realization that I had to follow my passion for pickleball. To help me decide where I was headed I made a conscious decision to just say "yes" to anything pickleball related and "no" to all other opportunities.

I'm a semi-retired energy practitioner In Kelowna, BC. One of my clients told me about pickleball. She said she was playing a few hours at a time. I honestly didn't believe her. She was in her 50s. There was a "learn to play" happening at the courts down the street from me. I was curious. I wanted to see what it was all about. I searched on the internet and found out when they were meeting. As soon as I started playing I fell in love with the game. I played my first tournament and decided I'd learn to be a ref so I could better understand the rules. I truly felt lost about the rules. I struggled to question calls. There were game-changing rallies that I wanted to know what was the correct call.

I got certified as a first level associate referee and continued playing. Then COVID hit. At the time I was hosting a holistic market and psychic fair. I was coming up to my fifth year anniversary organizing this successful and profitable event. It featured 50-plus vendors at eight events annually. Each event included high-quality vendors attracting nearly 600 people in attendance.

Due to COVID, the venue I booked shut down and did not reopen for two years. Initially I thought I'd just have to wait it out. Eventually I took the business to an online format which helped me get comfortable in front of a camera. I was able to work with fifteen vendors for an online holistic summit. We had more than 350 attendees online. I felt like this was a good compromise and a way to continue working.

I connected with people on an energetic level and was immersed in my practice. Connecting our community was what I did best. I helped vendors get exposure. It was a big launching pad for businesses and I was able to facilitate this. I was an energetic practitioner. My field included Shiatsu, Reiki energy healing, Shakra balancing and sound healing with Tibetan bowls.

However, as so many things were changing and getting canceled, I was unable to pull it together the next year. It was a very dark time for me. My work was my life, my heart, my passion. When that ended it took a piece of my soul. I lost my tribe. I lost my extended family. Suddenly I felt alone, I had nothing. I had to refund ten thousand dollars of deposits to vendors. Although I was able to get government support, financially I did not recover. I had to close everything down.

In the winter it is so dark here in Canada. The cloud cover just sits here. It is difficult for many of us to not be depressed in normal times. Even pickleball was shut down during the pandemic. We were not allowed to play. Spending time alone affected my mental health. Pickleball was something I had looked forward to and it helped my well-being. Now it was forbidden. If caught we would have faced fines of up to $2,000 for playing pickleball.

I decided to retrain myself. I took classes in course creation to utilize my knowledge as a practitioner. I learned how to do speaking engagements and coaching in my field. At the same time, a small group of us decided we would take our chances and go underground and play pickleball. Due to an auto-immune issue, I chose not to be vaccinated. This caused me a lot of grief and backlash in the community. I would be invited to a gathering and people wouldn't come because I was unvaccinated. People who I thought were friends stayed away from me. It hurt. Fortunately, there was a core group that included me and we met regularly to play.

Pickleball soon became more than a passion for me. I focused on sharing my holistic background with a pickleball twist. I turned my knowledge of acupressure and energy healing into courses and guidebooks to help with neck, shoulder, elbow and wrist pain for pickleball players. I established the ilovepickleball.ca website and developed a video channel and Facebook and Instagram accounts. Now I'm writing a book to accompany the courses. I speak at pickleball-related podcasts. I was featured as a guest speaker on 'The Pickleball Summit' with CJ Johnson and Tony Roig, 'Pickleball Fire Podcast' with Lynn Cherry and the 'Pickleball Happy Hour' with Dotti Berry. The topics have included: 'How to Get More Points by Connecting to your Pickleball Partner's Energy'; 'Funny Pickleball Scores' and '6 Easy Ways to Reduce Arm and Shoulder Pain'. I am also a volunteer moderator for the Pickleball Forum For Women

Happy Hour show. I am even included in this book about how pickleball empowers women!

In 2022 things started to open up again. I went to the local Kelowna Club to volunteer at an event. I mentioned to the organizers that I was looking for work. With more than 600 athletic members, they were looking to hire a paid contract person as a registrar. They hired me as the Registrar and Tournament Director of the Kelowna Club. I have also been commissioned to run tournaments at a neighboring club. Now I use my skill set to bring together the pickleball community instead of energy vendors. It suits me well.

I'm still climbing my way back up. Pickleball has been a lifesaver. It has, quite literally, changed my life and helped me with getting out from rock bottom. Pickleball has given me mental focus and clarity, helped me get back in physical shape, brought me a lot of fun, given me social connections and helped give me purpose and direction again. As I continue to evolve with this sport, it is also starting to give me income and career possibilities. I'm inspired. I have goals to bring Nationals to our club and much more. The pickleball passion has put a smile back on my face and given me a bright outlook for my future.

Roxanna Proczka

Pickleball as Medicine

I never played a racquet sport. I was into rock climbing and hiking. Having an outlet for my job as a nurse at an Arizona medical center was very important to me. It was 2020 and I needed a place to release all the stress from work. Many people were dealing with sadness, isolation and lacking joy. These past couple of years have been hard on the world.

A friend suggested a fairly new sport called pickleball. I said I'd give it a try. In the midst of the pandemic I started going to nearby Kleinman park. I had a positive experience, so after that first game I found a pickleball starter kit on Amazon. I started meeting so many interesting people. It reminds me of when you go to a bar and start seeing the regulars coming in. Little by little you all begin to know each other. Eventually relationships develop and deeper friendships. I knew I had connected when people started checking in to see when I was going to the courts.

I don't typically share a lot about myself. I am a strong, independent confident woman at school, work and as a daughter. I've never been one to show a lot of emotion. I'd say you can even call me stoic. So when my marriage began to unravel and I began to gain excessive weight, I kept it all to myself. During all the COVID stress at work, I got very out of shape. I was borderline obese. It greatly affected my relationship as well as my self-esteem.

Then, pickleball arrived. I really feel like it saved my life physically and mentally. I lost 40 pounds, learned to show my emotions and eventually felt comfortable to sharing my inner feelings with others. I learned how to express sadness, as well as happiness. With the weight loss I noticed diet was a huge factor. I started incorporating a better diet, and more nutrition awareness and became motivated to be better. In the beginning, pickleball was a struggle: I needed to drill, work on the game and develop some skills. Everyone I met was so kind, welcoming and open and made me feel OK to be vulnerable. The pickleball community provided me with a safe place.

At first I didn't want anyone to know what was going on in my personal life. I'm an aggressive player and hid behind that demeanor. But you could tell something was wrong with me. One day someone pulled me aside and asked, "Are you OK?" That kindness and simple question prompted me to open up and share the pain that I was in. A huge weight was lifted—both physically and emotionally. I had been playing five days a week to avoid emotions. I tried not to think about problems.

Ironically, even though it was my escape, pickleball was also a place that helped me face my problems. Since the beginning I have played more than 100 matches and won seventeen medals this past year. Realizing how beneficial the sport was for me, I decided to introduce it to my workplace. It has helped bridge and forge friendships at work. We started a monthly voluntary day to play and teach pickleball at the hospital. It is a thrill to see managers come out and to see the human side of workers. It has had a very positive effect on the work environment. Working on myself, feeling better and losing weight also has had a positive effect on my marriage.

Gratefully, we are back together and he has also become involved in the pickleball community. The big takeaway from all of these challenges for me was: Don't assume what people are thinking. You have to ask. It was the ask from that pickleball player, someone I barely knew, that put the positive change in motion.

Whether it's a marriage or a mixed doubles partner—we are all different. The communication may be different from one to another. I found I needed to better understand methods of communication. I just started to read the five love languages to help me learn the different ways people communicate. We tend to think everyone thinks just like us but they don't. This lesson applies not only in pickleball, but in everyday life. In my role as a nurse I have learned to ask, "Are you ok? Help me to understand what is going on." When someone asked that to me that first time at pickleball, my life turned around. I also learned that saying, "That's OK, no problem, let's focus on the next thing," can relieve tension and have a positive impact on situations.

Good communication skills are so vitally important for our well-being.

My pickleball game took off. I started competing in tournaments last summer. I signed up and played every single tournament in Arizona. I'm planning to be more selective this year and start playing some bigger tournaments. I drill a lot. My goal is to be a 4.5 or 5.0 level player. I'm currently at the 19+ 4.0 level. I started at 3.0 and within one year leveled up by drilling with partners, playing in leagues: both women's and mixed. I also watch a lot of sports, listen to feedback and learn a lot by watching online videos of pickleball lessons. I typically play 2-4 hours at a time. I watched Nationals in the desert and was so inspired that I made it a goal to get there.

To say I love to play is not even close to how I feel. My boss jokes that I better not go pro and leave my job. I love being a nurse and I love pickleball. It would be fun to get a sponsor. Being a nurse, I work in the healing profession. Interestingly, pickleball was the medicine that healed me.

I play at the Pickleball Kingdom, an indoor air conditioned gym with outdoor concrete courts. We can play all year round. I met my first pickleball friend there. She was the first one who got me into a tournament. She saw me transpire into a healthy life. If it was up to me, I'd have everyone try pickleball. I tell workers and friends to check it out. I give pickleball gifts for the holidays.

If pickleball can change my life so dramatically, I know it can help others. It's a sport for the whole family, all ages and all levels. Why not find a remedy for life that is a much easier pill to swallow than traditional medicine. And that's coming from a nurse.

Theresa Proud

WTF Pickleball (Where's The Fun)

It was an ordinary day with extraordinary results. It began in Omaha, Nebraska at the Common Ground Community Center in 2018. I was walking on the running track on the balcony above the basketball court when I noticed people playing an unusual game with paddles, a whiffle ball and a net. It didn't look like tennis, badminton or ping pong but I was intrigued. What kind of game are these old people playing? WTF (Where's The Fun?) Wow! They look like they really are having fun.

As a former Iowa girls' basketball player from 50 years ago (1973), I have always enjoyed sports, competition and physical activity. I asked some onlookers what type of game these old but active people were playing and they said, "Pickleball; You should try it." I didn't have any equipment, but the group was so welcoming that they let me borrow a paddle, got me in a game, gave me a short instruction lesson and I was hooked.

A few years later, when I moved to Montana with my husband, I didn't know anyone except my immediate family. In order to meet people and develop friendships, I immediately got involved with pickleball. It wasn't always easy to fit into some of the cliques. Most people were very welcoming, but there were a few people that would roll their eyes and forget that they too were once new to the game of pickleball. I've learned to appreciate the good people and karma will take care of the others.

I have invested my time and talents by sharing my love of pickleball with my husband, my children, my grandchildren, my siblings and friends. It's one of the best investments I've ever made. It's so much fun to travel in the U.S. and play pickleball with new people who become friends. Your "SHIP" will come in when you start playing pickleball. The wealth you receive may be in the following: CompanionSHIP, FriendSHIP, PartnerSHIP, RelationSHIP, and CourtSHIP. Pickleball is not a game of being perfect. It's a game of progress. You either win or you learn in a game. In pickleball I strive for progress, not perfection. WTF: Where's The Fun? It's clear it's in playing pickleball.

Sonia Quiz

Winning by Losing

I know I sound dramatic when I say pickleball saved my life. It's the absolute truth. About ten years ago I was in a really bad place mentally. I live in a small town called Fowler in California. I had two small children and an alcoholic, drug-addicted abusive spouse. He chose other women and drugs over me. I became a shut-in, I wouldn't leave my house. I began eating to cope with the stress. Food gave me comfort and helped me numb myself. I went from a relatively fit athletic person to 315 pounds. I became deeply depressed. I considered taking my life. But I had two children to live for and knew I had to stay alive.

One day when dropping off my son at school I noticed these weird-looking courts. It took me about a year to work up the courage to check them out. At that time my state of mind was at my lowest point. I felt the world would be better off without me. I asked them what sport they were playing. They were all so friendly and immediately invited me to play.

My high school counselor and the parents of friends were there playing. That was the best week of my life. I kept going back every day. It wasn't easy at first as my weight was an issue. After a couple of months I started noticing that feeling of anticipation and happiness. It was 2014, I was at my highest weight when I found pickleball. I was motivated to eat healthier, be better, play better, to get in shape. I wanted to be like the other players. I wanted to have the mobility and stamina to play. I started walking, paying attention to my food intake and feeling encouraged.

A friend said I needed to get a shirt that says "one more game" as I spent 3-4 hours per day on the courts. It really saved my life. I began to find my courage and strength and remember who I was. I used to be naturally outgoing and loved being around people. Pickleball awoke me to myself. Suddenly I had friends, was texting and making lunch dates and traveling. I went to tournaments and had the time of my life.

I realized I didn't need to take the abuse anymore. I asked my husband to leave. Thankfully, he did. By 2015 I was down to 148 pounds and feeling really happy. I met my new husband that same year. He had two small children for whom he was the sole parent. I raised his children as mine. I slowly started gaining the weight back. This time it was not from depression, just lack of exercise. I was happy, but I was not taking care of myself physically. My husband is a chef. We were eating late and eating well. By 2019 I was back up to 300 pounds. I saw it happening, but didn't care. He asked me to marry him when I was at my heaviest. The weight was never an issue between us. The problem was that I was in bad health, I had very high blood pressure, diabetes, stage two cirrhosis of the liver and kidney disease. This was all from eating poorly and drinking alcohol.

We got married in 2019. When I found out my oldest son and his wife were going to have a baby, I realized I needed to get in shape. I decided to get a gastric sleeve in 2021. The younger children were old enough now for me to get back on the courts. As soon as I was cleared to exercise I went back to playing pickleball again. I once again found so much happiness in making many new friendships. The kids now play with me. We all started playing in tournaments.

By 2022 I had lost all the weight and was down to 125 pounds. For two years now I no longer drink alcohol or carbonated beverages.Today I am feeling the confidence that I had lost. I know I can do things to make myself happy and I don't have to settle for less. I was hired to a full-time job for the first time in 24 years. It has cut into my pickleball time, but pickleball remains a priority for me.

At first my husband had a hard time adjusting to my dramatic changes. It was a bit rocky at first. There were so many changes: my new job, my new friends, my new weight. His job situation will be changing soon and he is going to start playing pickleball with me. I'm looking forward to us sharing that together.

I am grateful to say that the pickleball people never treated me any differently throughout my many stages. I stayed the same and people were able to see me for who I really am. I probably have over 200 people in my cell with the last name "Pickleball." I don't see myself ever quitting pickleball. I love playing and exercising. I can get up, move, and do things that I couldn't do before. I was motivated to stop getting hit unintentionally—by the ball by 80-year-olds. I was just slow to move when I was overweight.

I started playing at different locations and going to tournaments where I was meeting so many amazing people. I currently play at the 4.0 level. My goal is to one day be at the pro level. I would love to play in the Olympics. I used to be embarrassed to say my age, but now I can't wait to be 50 so I can play in the senior bracket. I like to drill, work on shots, encourage people and teach others to play. I do squats, jog and keep moving. I'm very competitive. I work hard on having a good attitude, but occasionally I do lose my temper, although I never stay in that anger very long. I always encourage everyone to come check out pickleball. I tell them they just cannot come and blame me when they get addicted to the sport.

I have gained friends and lost 190 pounds.

I don't take any more medicine for my high blood pressure. My liver, kidneys and heart are in perfect health. I am no longer diabetic. I was on a path of self-destruction. Now I'm on the path to winning another gold medal in a tournament this weekend. I play with great friends that no longer have the last name "Pickleball", now they are just friends in my contacts.

We are a close family. I was always careful not to use body-shaming language around my children. They all encouraged me to get active. They are all into fitness. My kids enjoy playing. We made a t-shirt for my 10-year-old daughter that says future gold pickleballer. My 14-year-old son is playing and wants to become better so we can be partners in future tournaments. It has become a family bonding event. We are all having a great time. Pickleball saved me in more ways than one. And it has reminded me of who I am. It broke me out of my shell that I was in for more than 15 years—depressed and lonely. Not to mention, the doctor told me I would die if I didn't take my health seriously.

I've been playing now for a few years with a group of friends. They invited me to play out of state and as a gift, they all pitched in to buy my plane ticket. How amazing is that! I absolutely love this sport and I am so blessed to have met all these wonderful friends.

Leslie Roberts 

Bulletproofing the Body

I live in Austin, Texas, but where I'm from could not be more different. I grew up in a tiny town in Kansas made up of three mostly dirt streets. I walked or biked to school and never once owned a bike lock. The culture of those days was simple and as kids, we played outside until forced to go inside.

I was a crazy, feral child with zero governance. My parents were divorced and my mother was an absent alcoholic dating a married man who lived with his wife a few houses away. By association, I had a reputation that I knew nothing about. Friends were not allowed to invite me over. My father lived about 40 minutes away and would support me financially for all of my childhood. On weekends, he would take me into the big city for lunch at a nice restaurant, to shop, see a movie. He taught me to drive when I was 12 and bought me my first car at 14 years old. As a teen, not only was I feral but now I was also independent.

Through this chaotic childhood, team sports were my savior. At one point, I played every sport available in my small town. Looking back, had the right sport been available to me, like gymnastics or golf, I could've been a standout. In my mid-20's a pro sports opportunity came up–I was recruited to play women's professional football. I wasn't great, clunking along in equipment made for men with my tiny 5'0" frame wasn't the easiest, but I'm happy for the experience. In my early 30's and in the early days of its inception, I became a competitive Crossfitter. It was fun and great for friendships, however brutal on the body.. No sport was more loved by me than doubles beach volleyball. It jived with my ethos. I spent many, many hours (have been spent) training and playing in the sand, but my height would never warrant a truly competitive level.

One day in a park while walking my dogs, I saw Pickleball for the first time and asked what they were playing. It would be two years before I would play Pickleball for the first time, in the summer of 2020. I signed up for a new league, bought a $35 Amazon paddle and strained my calf wearing the wrong shoes in the first session. No matter, I was instantly smitten.

I remember the exact moment, just a couple of months into playing, this mid-game realization that my short stature may not be an obstacle to achieving a high level of skill. It was in that very moment that I decided to put my best efforts into the growth of my game. I started taking lessons and upgraded my paddle.

About five months later, something very important would happen. A local clinic was going to be taught by a pro player. I'd never met or seen pro play before. I was just starting to watch some videos. I signed up for the clinic with Zane Navratil and waited three long months.

I was close to a 4.0 level when the clinic came around, as I had been drilling and taking regular lessons. Zane was polite, very kind and we had a common connection—he's from a small town, too, and I just happen to have prominent fitness clients who live in his hometown who he knows. We played a few points together and I noticed a little hitch in his get up—a famed Texas saying—so I offered, "hey, I can help you with that!" and he was interested in hearing what I had to say, because unbeknownst to me, he was at the stage in his career where he was building a team. He was ready for a fitness coach. He wanted a coach who played pickleball and understood what his body was going through on the court. We agreed to help each other and that simple meeting set me on the trajectory of where I am today.

Pickleball is simply one of the most fun, addictive activities to which I've ever been introduced. I am the type to attempt to master a skill I find interesting and not grow bored of the grind to attain that mastery. I love details. Taking my childhood into account, the only discipline I've ever known has been from sport. It's still my savior to this day.

To be blunt, the course of my life could've easily been like many others in my small town—never leaving, marrying early, high school pregnancies and using drugs. I credit sports for what my charmed life has been. I became a fitness trainer at the age of 22. I have a lot of curiosity to explore and instead of exploring things that would bring me down, I explored the things that have brought me up. Now I dedicate this ethos to others. I help clients to explore the new and maybe find a new love. I've introduced some now addicts to pickleball. I gave a first lesson to a group of women in their 70's who have been my fitness clients for four years. They messaged me a few hours later that they bought their first paddles.

Pickleball is special as it continues to help me grow in a physical and mental sense. It's difficult to master and I'm learning from the ground up. Hitting a slice is something I had never done before. That damn shot is my nemesis. I'd say the only sport I ever found this difficult is golf. But pickleball is just as, if not more, gratifying when solving the chess like strategy that gets you a win.

I love the partner element and that it just takes four people for a game. I have work to do when it comes to trust. Having a partner I trust is a wonderful feeling. I hope that pickleball helps me find more people who understand that aspect of my personality. I'm extroverted, easy to talk to, I want to help others succeed, but I don't trust easily. It's a confident person who can walk up to a person they've never met, stick out their hand and introduce themselves. Pickleball is powerful in helping people develop healthy human connections via that simple hello.

As for game growth, I'm feeling that it becomes a bit of up and down. I've now medaled at the 5.0 level. I am the only woman to make it to the semi finals in a very male dominated inaugural Minor League Pickleball 22 division tournament that took place in October 2022. Minors is the same format as Major League Pickleball. The rally and team format is by far the most fun I've ever had playing pickleball. I hope for many more of these opportunities in my future.

These days I'm the fitness coach for several players on the professional tour, having helped a few top ten players play at their best. I help amateur players grow their game as a certified coach and, as a trainer, reduce their risk of injury. I love to, as my business name implies, bulletproof the body. I hope to do this within pickleball for many more years to come.

Judith Roth

Success Using the Beginner's Mind

My Aikido teacher saw me struggling. He said "You need to completely let go of your previous action and meet the moment with a fresh mind. Let each response go and be present for the next move." At the time I had no idea that his words of wisdom would one day serve me as a pickleball player.

I was over 70 years old when I was introduced to pickleball. I not only had zero court experience, but I didn't even know how to hold a racket. It was daunting! Unfortunately, my excitement for this new sport was quickly put on hold once the pandemic hit. After sheltering for more than a year, I was grateful to begin playing again at the local YMCA. I felt intimidated due to my lack of experience. Fortunately, I was able to draw from the life skill I learned forty years ago from my Aikido instructor.

My sensei (teacher) talked about "the beginner's mind" as the ultimate attitude to which we must aspire. At first, this confused me. As a beginner in Aikido I felt clumsy and fearful as I trained with experienced black belts. I was feeling "less than" while the teacher was describing "the beginner's mind" as the highest evolution of attitude. Through training, I began to understand what this meant.

At first, while learning the art of Aikido, I found myself unable to respond as my teacher had demonstrated. My male partner approached me with an extended arm in a striking pose, I recoiled in fear and frustration. I had to let go of all the things the opponent inside of me was saying. "You don't know what you're doing and you'll never be able to respond effectively."

In time, I began to understand what the teachers were talking about when they told us to invite and live in "the beginner's mind." This meant quieting my mind, letting go of the opponent within, giving myself full permission to try something, not judging or categorizing my actions, but instead bringing myself completely and fully to the next moment and liberating myself to be a fresh beginner.

This profound teaching was deeply impactful. The "beginner's mind" was useful as I moved into each evolution in my life. I moved to new places I'd never lived and created new work I'd never done by internalizing and embracing this powerful attitude. I learned how to overcome the opponent living inside of me. I went on to get my black belt and to create a women's non-profit organization in Seattle teaching full-force self-defense and empowerment. I led an international fundraiser collecting over $100,000 dollars for women survivors of the Bosnian war and took women's empowerment workshops to Croatia. I built a home yoga studio in Seattle and created a community of neighbors learning yoga. I moved to a village in Mexico, learned Spanish, built a yoga temple and brought a yoga economy to the village. All of these leaps of faith were guided by the power of the "beginner's mind."

Then I was introduced to pickleball. Using the "beginner's mind" I viewed my success not by winning or losing, but instead by choosing a focus of skill development. I began by focusing on my serve. In time, my serve became more consistent and each successful serve proved a win for me.

As a new pickleball player, I went to a local athletic club looking to find games. Several guys had been playing and were sitting around and preparing to leave. I nervously asked if anyone wanted to play. They saw I was a new player ,and I knew they really didn't want to play with me. Then a man with a strong tennis background said, "I'll play with you. I want to practice my serves." I said "ok." I had no idea what I was in for.

He hit one strong serve after another at me. My opponent within started yelling; "Hey don't play with this guy. He is thrashing you. You'll never be able to return his serves." I started breathing deeply into everything I ever learned about the "beginner's mind." I welcomed each of his forceful serves. I let each miss go and brought myself to the next one. In time, I found myself returning all his serves. As a result, I am now confident in returning the most challenging serves.

At the beginning of each game I choose one simple focus. Sometimes it's as simple as "Keep your eye on the ball," "Return the serve deep," or "Let your opponent make the mistakes." Other reminders I use are: return low, place drop shots instead of slamming the ball, slow the game down, be patient, place your dink at an angle, move your opponents, create openings, and send the ball through the openings. I find that I gain more skills by just using one focus at a time. My personal wins have increased as my focus has sharpened.

Recently I teamed up with a man I'd never played with before. I had played against him so I knew he was a strong player. I watched as his inner opponent took over his game. He was saying out loud: "I'm having a bad day. I just can't seem to hit the ball. I keep missing those shots. Nothing is going right for me. It's one of those days." I decided to focus on staying light, enjoying the play and smiling. This kept me from being affected by the wild balls he hit into the net. Instead, I cherished each opportunity to serve, each chance to return, each time I got to dink or drop a ball and change the pace of the game. We may have lost the games but I was winning, while his inner opponent was causing him to lose. As we left the courts that day, I had a number of players remark "You have a great attitude." I'd never really heard that from other players before. I was not surprised by the comments because I had intentionally used my attitude to focus and not engage with my partner's issues.

Using the "beginner's mind" once again created my personal win. I am forever grateful for the ability to not only continue to play pickleball, but to thoroughly enjoy the sport with a positive mind and continued good results.

Erin Sataloff 

A Solid Tribe in Pickleball

My life has had major significant events. My grandfather committed suicide when I was a kid. I joined the Army. I survived cancer. I got married and divorced and I was a step parent. However, one of the biggest life-changing things that have led to my new life, was a singular instance of domestic violence.

My most recent long-term relationship ended in the summer of 2019 after 12 years on and off. About a year and a half before I left, my partner and I got into a disagreement and he ended up striking me multiple times. I didn't leave then, but the relationship was never the same. Once I finally decided to leave, I put all my belongings into storage, packed up my pets, drove to Los Angeles and began picking up the pieces of my life.

I was born and raised in Los Angeles, but spent a lot of time out of state in my 20s and early 30s. I joined the army when I was 20. I studied

Arabic and became a translator. Then I got thyroid cancer at 22 while on active duty and lived in Germany for three years.

I left the military after more than five years, spent a year in Los Angeles, and then moved to Washington State. I went to the University of Washington, where I graduated Summa Cum Laude with a 4.0 GPA and a Bachelor's Degree in Psychology. I went to UC Davis for one year of a PhD program but it didn't make me happy, so I moved back to Washington. I worked full-time at a middle school but still was unable to feel happiness. I was in a lot of chronic pain and was diagnosed with fibromyalgia.

I moved back to Los Angeles (just before COVID shut everything down). I have always needed to stay active for my body to feel good, so I never went back to a desk job. I was single and back "home" and couldn’t figure out what would make me happy. All I knew for sure is that my life revolved around my family, friends, and pets. I was also doing pottery as my main hobby, but I still wasn't fulfilled.

At the end of summer 2020, everything was completely locked down. My mom and I wanted to play tennis, so we started taking some lessons at our local park. Unfortunately my mom injured her shoulder so we stopped the lessons. Luckily I had watched some people playing a different game on a smaller net and it looked so fun. I approached them and asked if I could try, since I didn't have a tennis partner anymore. They graciously welcomed me. I immediately bought a starter paddle (which I almost also broke immediately) and jumped in with both feet.

I took a few lessons with a local coach and decided I wanted to try to play some tournaments. I was very excited and ambitious. I had never done competitive team-based sports other than playing AYSO soccer very badly. I was a horse person through and through, but this sport was different. The first "different" thing about pickleball is the people. I had been gone from California for around six years and hadn't established a solid tribe. Within two weeks of discovering pickleball, I had a tribe that literally met to play all day, every day. We were all always ready to play no matter what.

Before pickleball, I was active for an hour here and there, maybe I'd go to the gym or maybe for a walk. After I started playing pickleball I found I could be active for three to five hours. The most significant change is my work status. I am a 100% disabled veteran and never thought I would be able to work consistently again. Sitting in an office literally tortured my body and made me depressed. But outside on the pickleball court I am now coaching and my body is lightly active all day. I'm focused on something I truly enjoy doing.

Pickleball has been life-changing physically and mentally and it's given me a purpose. It's given me personal goals, friendships, better body coordination, motivation to get up early, the thrill of competition and the pride of success. There are a million ways in which my life has improved since discovering this amazing sport. Pickleball has become the missing piece for me. I finally created a lifestyle doing something that genuinely makes me happy. I started out playing with the intent of having fun and getting exercise, but coaching has given me a sense of purpose and fulfillment. Helping others feel confident and capable is so rewarding to me.

My military service, having cancer, and then having permanent disabilities/injuries made me feel like playing a sport wasn't a realistic option for me. Because of the size of the court and the size and weight of the paddle, pickleball made me feel like I could be competitive again.

Now I feel even more capable than I did even during military service. There was a time I was feeling hopeless, back in Los Angeles, feeling alone. Pickleball has changed all that. It is something to look forward to every day.

This sport can be played by almost every person, regardless of age, gender, mobility, etc. I can play with my 87-year-old grandma or my neighbor's seven-year-old granddaughter. It is accessible to everyone. I see the goodness in what it can bring to someone's life. My pickleball tribe has brought much goodness to mine.

Lauren Sibley

Healing Through Pickleball

I think it was about 4 years ago (2019) that I picked up my first pickleball paddle. One of those nice, heavy wood ones, that I had borrowed from a friend. My mom had invited me to play with a group of women from her neighborhood. I couldn't play often because they got together in the morning and I was living about 30 minutes away going to college and working. During that same year my husband and I found out that I was pregnant with our first child, after the first trimester I stopped playing all together.

At the beginning of February 2020, my life changed dramatically. Some intense highs and lows ensued. It began with the birth of our son, who is the most energetic little human on this earth. His birth was rough on me physically and mentally. Labor itself was a 32-hour ordeal that left me completely exhausted. A few hours after his birth we found out that my bladder had sustained major damage during labor and delivery and was not functioning. In addition to this, I had an allergic reaction to the adhesive used for the epidural, which resulted in hives breaking out all over my back. This caused more than just physical pain, the mental toll was unbearable. Because of the rash I was not able to sleep, the pain in my back was too intense.

I was connected to a catheter, since my bladder wasn't functioning.

I was not able to hold my baby. To walk from room to room I had to carry an external bladder instead of my new baby boy. Bladders actually must heal on their own, and so we had to wait. The waiting led to many tear-filled nights as it seemed there was no end in sight to this problem. It took two weeks, eight catheters, one bladder infection, and 1 yeast infection, then I could finally move around untethered and things slowly started to look up.

Following the two weeks that it took to heal my bladder, I returned to my college classes for my last semester. I only had two classes and two months left for my Bachelor's degree. Unfortunately, this didn't last long. We had heard whisperings of a virus far away in China, it seemed like all of the sudden it was here in the US, and then my life which had already changed, was changing again. Our classes were moved online and the world shut down for "two weeks," which we all know turned into much longer.

My nights were once more filled with tears as I felt trapped and scared. One of the biggest suggestions for women who have recently given birth, is to get out and be social, because that helps prevent and mitigate postpartum depression and anxiety. With social distancing in place my postpartum depression and anxiety elevated. It felt like I was terrified of everything and that I couldn't reason with myself. I often felt that I was going insane because fear beat out reason every time. As the weather began to warm up, it was encouraged that we spend time outside if we were going to be with people. My mom and her group began playing pickleball again. Since I was now finished with school and really didn't have much to do I began to drive the 30 minutes every morning to my parent's house. My dad would take my son on a walk while my mom and I played. I was terrible and couldn't figure out how to control the ball and make it do what I wanted it to do. But it became a motivating thing for me. I loved the sport and wanted to improve so badly. I would sit and watch high-level players at the parks and on Youtube and try to replicate their form and shots.

My husband saw me come alive again and gain some passion back in my life. For my birthday in 2020 he bought me a new Franklin Paddle and a bag. The new gear got me even more motivated, prompting me to take lessons and classes. After graduating college I felt like I had lost myself, I had no goals and nothing to work towards. Pickleball was the path that brought me back to myself. It also gave me a social network, which had been dwindling for many years.

Naturally shy and introverted I was never very outgoing, but playing pickleball gave me a way to make friends. Some of my deepest friendships have been built around this sport and I love it for that. To say that it saved my life, I feel is an understatement. I am scared to even imagine where I would be without pickleball. It was my only weapon to combat the dragon of postpartum depression and anxiety. It brought motivation and passion back to my life when I thought there wasn't much going on for me anymore. It brought me a social network, a hobby, and even a job.

I have been able to develop a good group of students in my new town, and I am able to play and teach throughout the week. I love every chance I get to play and I love all the people I get to meet. Yes, it's fair to say that pickleball saved my life.

Helle Sparre 

From a Tennis Ball to a Pickleball

For 50 years tennis was my main sport. I was a junior champion in Denmark, played open-era Wimbledon, taught tennis at clubs in the U.S. and wrote a book about tennis strategy. So it was quite a surprise when at age 60, I stumbled upon a very unique game called pickleball.

I was visiting a tennis friend who was a student at Chico State. We had just finished playing tennis and were walking out from the courts. A woman much older than us (and we were no spring chickens) approached us with a comforting enthusiastic smile and asked us to follow her. She was carrying some sort of props that were used for making a court in the middle of a flat asphalt area. Soon after, a fourth person showed up. That was my first game of pickleball. I was thinking: "What is this? It can't be that difficult! Is it mini tennis like I played in my junior days?" This sport involves touch, movement, power, thinking ahead and quick reflexes, just to mention a few. These were all my favorite things from my love for tennis, right here on the tiny pickleball court.

We were told the basic rules, however, as a tennis player I continued to serve and volley. I had to be reminded to let the return bounce. Everybody laughed at these silly rules. The kitchen line was hard to respect. I was repeatedly called for no volley zone (NVZ) foot-fault violations. Then the crazy scoring got me shaking my head in disbelief. It took nearly five months before I really began to grasp the scorekeeping.

Something very social, playful, fun, challenging and addictive was awakened in me. That was my introduction to pickleball back in 2015. Shortly after, I moved to Arizona where it was already popular. Teaching tennis was still my main work but pickleball soon began taking up more and more of my time. This new sport was challenging both physically and mentally. I felt like a kid again. I got to hit drop shots, swinging volleys and smashing balls hard back and forth during every point, shots that were considered rare and low percentage in tennis.

The book I had written for tennis was called ***Dynamite Doubles, Play Winning Tennis Today!*** and details doubles strategies such as partnership, court positioning and shot selection. I soon realized the same system of court coverage, teamwork, and player responsibilities would work wonders for pickleball—with of course a slight tweaking to fit the pickleball court game and rules.

One thing led to another, and now six years later I've now played and won tournaments all over the states with many wonderful partners and met incredibly interesting fun like-minded people. The social aspect of pickleball is very different from tennis. I appreciate all the friends I have made through pickleball.

Dynamite Doubles for Pickleball is now an online course and has been received better than I could have ever expected. The vision I had with ***Dynamite Doubles for Tennis*** has now manifested in the pickleball world and I am so incredibly grateful for all the support I am receiving from students and players all over the world. Three years ago I was able to introduce ***Dynamite Doubles for Pickleball*** to college students in Thailand. I am also excited to be part of "ALL IN YOUTH" Pickleball out of Tucson, to teach pickleball through several organizations that serve kids in need and eventually take them to pickleball tournaments.

More and more pro and college tennis players are coming over to pickleball. We have just barely scratched the surface of where this game is going. New shots and new moves are being created every day and there is no limit to where things will go. It's a very exciting time and every single day new players are introduced to this game and get hooked! Finally, a healthy addiction.

In 2022 I started offering a Dynamite Doubles Coaches Certification program (DDCC) so we can continue to teach more players how to play smarter, not harder pickleball while having fun and socializing, keeping us young and healthy. We currently have more than 25 certified Dynamite Doubles coaches all over the U.S. which makes my heart smile and fills me with gratitude.

I was here in the 1970s for the beginning of Women's Pro Tennis and the forming of the WTA and now almost 50 Years later here I am at the grassroots for pickleball. With my new career I am excited to be part of the fastest growing sport in America. As we all continue to grow in this sport, I encourage everyone to help widen this circle of pickleball love.

Aubri Steele

A Brand New Civility

Parenting through the pandemic was further challenged by the divisive behaviors running rampant throughout our Country. It felt impossible to stand firmly behind the beliefs on which I was raised. The instructions of our parents to "play nicely" seemed all but lost as the world clumsily navigated through 2020. How could we possibly ask civility of our children when the world at large was slipping ever so swiftly into a pattern where manners didn't matter and the rigidity of beliefs was provoking controversy, inappropriate behavior, and a seemingly infectious absence of empathy.

This is not a political statement, this is a reflection of the human experience. As a human race, it seemed we were losing our way. As a parent, this was a heartbreaking glimpse into a future I did not want for my children.

On a whim, my husband decided to paint a pickleball court in the front driveway. It seemed fun but insignificant at the time. Knowing little about the sport, we thought it would be a way to engage our five teenage children and keep them active amid the closure of schools, sports, and their social lives.

We were familiar with pickleball as a sport our parents and their friends were playing.The smaller court and dink-style play allowed for varying levels of exertion, and was accessible for people of all ages. We quickly became well-versed in the game and began inviting neighbors and friends to play, all while maintaining social distance and excessive sanitizing of equipment. We enjoyed pickleball as a sport that we could play with both our parents and our children. Birthdays and holidays in 2020 were spent eating outdoors and rotating through a few games of pickleball. It was the perfect way to bring our family together.

As a child of an entrepreneurial father, I was raised in his small manufacturing business in Burbank, California. Even though Dad was a college dropout, he saw a need in the semiconductor industry and took a chance. Some of my earliest memories were time spent in the office where my mom did the books. Still today, the smell of cut metal from the machine shop lingers delicately in the corners of my conscience.

Throughout the 28 years that Dad ran his company, I watched as he employed everyone in our family, most of our extended family, all of his brothers, many of their wives, children and siblings. He built success stories from high school graduates, and sent many of his employee's children to college. He donated millions to charity, and truly enriched the lives of everyone he touched. I watched, in awe and admiration, as he built his metaphorical boat, loaded us all inside, and led us to a brighter future.

As you can imagine, when my father succumbed to his battle with cancer on August 28, 2020, that vessel came crashing onto a desolate and unfriendly shore. For months, I lay on that shore, angry and consumed by the loss of the greatest man I had ever known. Staring frustratingly at the fragments of wreckage littering the space around me, I wanted desperately to create a legacy in the way that he had, but felt so ill-equipped to do so and so paralyzed by devastation I could not escape.

That's when I started to realize that the pieces of wood now scattered around me, were the parts with which I could build my own boat and hopefully keep his legacy alive.

I noticed that there were no urban-facing apparel brands that married my active lifestyle with who I am as a woman. I couldn't find anything out there that felt as multifaceted as I do. I started thinking about a clothing line that would feature designs suitable for going from my office to the pickleball court, to the store, golfing with my husband, and maybe out for drinks, all with a great performance fabric fashion piece as the base. Thus was born Civile Apparel, a female-founded and run company. At Civile Apparel we see pickleball as a unifying sport that offers an accessible, fun, and competitive outdoor respite. Our clothing line makes it fashionable.

We look to where we are going by honoring where we came from. I am forever grateful for the guidance and remarkable power of a healthy relationship between a father and his daughter. Of all of my goals with Civile Apparel the biggest of these is to build a "boat" which will carry people to a better place, rise with the tide, house families, teach them to sail, and bring us all to a brighter destination. These were the lessons I learned from my father. I dedicate my company to his memory.

Susan Swern

Pickleball for Good

I have always loved participating in sports. Growing up, I was athletic and coordinated. My dad introduced me to tennis, skiing, table tennis and golf. My elementary gym teacher recruited me for every team, including basketball, volleyball and even field hockey. In 6th grade I won an all-around athlete award from my school district, though I never considered myself a star athlete. I simply loved to play, to be part of a team and compete.

As time went on, I gravitated towards racquet sports mostly to keep active and fit, enjoy the outdoors, and engage my competitive side. In recent years, my physical activities have been hampered by a variety of sports and non-sports related accidents. Like so many of us in our 50s and 60s+, I've adopted a feel-the-pain-and-do-it-anyway attitude or just shifted to less intensive sports and fitness outlets. In 2016 a dear friend of mine, Dede Frain, invited me to play pickleball for the first time at a local rec center. She is, by the way, another empowered woman who founded Babes Around Denver, the largest and longest running monthly women's party in the U.S. Dede sold me on the fact that I'd be a natural, and indeed, it was fun and fairly easy to get the hang of the basics (sans the scoring). Yet my first love was still tennis.

Then the COVID pandemic hit in March 2020. Friends of mine, all women and self-named the OGs (Original Gangsters), lured me out of my isolation and social coma to start having fun again in a very different type of kitchen than the one I cooked in. As more friends wanted to join us in pickleball, I launched a Facebook group on July 14, 2021, initially with 20 followers. I invited a friend, Kim Copeland, to join the OGs and me on the courts. Kim and I had already started discussing teaming up to find a way to do well while doing good–something that could naturally tap into our respective passions, strengths and values, as well as those in our circles. As we became increasingly passionate about pickleball, a lightbulb went off. Let's start an official club by and for the LGBTQ+Friends community, one that embodies our deepest ideals of inclusion, connection, safety, fitness, environmental sustainability and empowerment. And so, the Lavender Pickleball Club was born.

We chose the name because the color had become a symbol of diversity and LGBTQ+ empowerment, rights, pride, resistance, inclusion, even culture and fashion. We wanted everyone to feel welcome, regardless of level of play, sports ability, fitness AND identity. It quickly became apparent that this sport was so much more than physical activity and game. It is a game-changer. Our club became a catalyst for love, connection, acceptance, wellbeing and pride, on and off the court along with a ton of smiles and laughter.

What started with 20 Facebook followers has since grown to over 1,800 and 400+ annual members in 18 months. Since our founding, we've hosted two Outrageously Fun Fall Tournaments in Arvada, Colorado;

assembled a dedicated team of volunteer ambassadors who host drop-in and round robin play in the Denver Metro area; organized two professional clinics– one led by Irina Tereschenko, five time Grand Slam pickleball winner and Major League Pickleball favorite and another by Helle Sparre, one of the best pickleball instructors in the U.S. who teaches her patented Dynamite Doubles system; launched a LPC chapter in Palm Creek, Arizona; and had our story spotlighted in InPickleball Magazine and a segment on Denver 9 News Fair Game. LPC has served as an ambassador to introduce many new players to the sport, to help level up skills and to create a welcoming tribe and vibe. As inspiring as this sport and club had become to me, another idea started bubbling in my heart, mind and soul, one which tapped into another love, and my career calling, philanthropy.

For more than 35 years I've served in the philanthropic sector, as a development director, philanthropic partnerships officer and consultant. I am now thrilled to share a new venture Pickleball for Good™. Our mission is to unleash the power of pickleball for the benefit of all. We are dedicated to mobilizing resources for those who live in underserved and under resourced communities around the world. Financial resources, such as grants, matching funds, incentives and sponsorships will be awarded to vetted groups, organizations, clubs and schools. Equipment, gear, courts, and apparel—new and repurposed—will be collected and distributed.

At the core of Pickleball for Good are values which I've learned and cultivated throughout my lifetime, ones which embody the principles this sport can stand for: Sustainability, Equitability, Respect, Vision and Engagement. Our GoGreen initiative will support grantees to develop sustainable practices in the industry. I absolutely believe pickleball unites us more than divides, is the great equalizer and promotes unique social good. I believe pickleball can save America, democracy and, yes, even the world. Pickleball has been a complete game changer for me.

One of the first things I ask people I meet through pickleball is, "What is your pickleball story?" At the heart of my own pickleball love affair and story is its evolution from just another racquet sport to a life changing empowering vehicle for change, Through the launch of my two pickleball organizations—Lavender Pickleball Club and Pickleball for Good™, I continue to give and get much goodness in return.

Lee Whitwell

A Front Row Seat to the Game

I grew up in Gibraltar. My last two years of high school were spent in England where I learned to play tennis. In 1993, I moved to the United States to play tennis and volleyball in college. For a short time, I played pro tennis and then decided to get my master's degree. During that time I continued to play doubles and coach college-level tennis while attending Alliant International University in California, studying Industrial Organizational Psychology. I continued teaching on the resort side of things, however, I just wanted to play for fun at the club. Eventually, I became the director of tennis and fitness and teaching and running resort programs.

My partner and I decided to move to Bend, Oregon in 2015. We've been together a long time, more than 15 years. She gives me strength and support and is simply amazing. When we got to Bend, my friend Lisa Palcac asked me to play in a tournament. I mistakenly thought it was a tennis tournament. But then I found out it was pickleball. I was not interested. She tried to bribe me. I said, "Thanks, no thanks." Back then we all thought it was a sport for old people. So she upped the ante. The kicker was she offered me a case of beer if I would play. Naturally, I said, "I'm in."

I borrowed a paddle and didn't even know the rules. It was a local tournament in La Pine, Oregon. It was a blast. We won the tournament. I never would have imagined in my wildest of dreams how much fun that would be. I was hooked from that very first day. What struck me most was the warm feeling of community. There was a sense of social identity and that fabric was woven throughout those involved in the sport. It was bringing everyone together.

I believe the one thing that is hard to do in life, in sports, and even at work, is to easily make friendships. This is even more true as we age. Then along comes pickleball, providing a networking space where you end up with 300 new friends you didn't know you needed or wanted. Moreover, those friends come from as diverse a population as you can imagine.

Pickleball attracts all walks of life, all ages, all colors, all religions, all abilities, all beliefs, yet we all come together and play the game. No one is asking where you went to school or what job you have, it doesn't matter. What matters is that we are out there finding enjoyment together.

After that first tournament, I immediately signed up for another one. I owe it all to Lisa. She was teaching pickleball and brought me in. I had the good fortune of starting at a 5.0 level due to my years of tennis training. Lisa and I taught, did camps and played tournaments together. I eventually had the opportunity to help design and build a 10-court facility in Bend.

My life was more and more influenced by pickleball, although I continued to teach tennis at that time. The health benefits of pickleball are numerous. Many people who struggle with health issues find solace and distraction in playing. I know this first hand. I was diagnosed with Trigeminal neuralgia (TN), also known as tic douloureux. It is a type of chronic pain disorder that involves sudden, severe facial pain. It affects the trigeminal nerve, or fifth cranial nerve, which provides feeling and nerve signaling to many parts of the head and face. It is also known to some as the suicide disease. It is life-changing and life-altering.

Right before my 13th birthday I began experiencing extreme pain. I couldn't tell what was going on. I thought maybe it was TMJ (lockjaw) or a problem with my teeth. Fortunately my doctor was relentless and quickly figured out the problem. We tried to control it with medication, but nothing worked. It's sort of like a brain freeze that I feel all the time.

I've had six brain surgeries to date. It turns out I am one of the very few who cannot find relief. I have come to realize that I have no choice but to persevere with this disease. Although I continue to look for solutions, I am one of the rare cases that doesn't respond to medication. I have bilateral pain and all three types of pain associated with the disease. This is unusual. Very few people have the disease to this extent.

There are some new treatments, but I won't be a guinea pig and let them experiment on me. Sometimes my head feels like it's being shrunk in a vice, or someone is stabbing my ear canal with an ice pick, or I feel ants running through my face. Typically the disease is more common in the over-60 population. They simply don't understand why it occurs and why it happened to me.

I attended a support group for a while, but they were resigned to the illness. I decided I would own it and it would never own me. My attitude is to embrace my life and learn to live with my symptoms. Pickleball has been a tremendous source of relief and distraction. When I'm playing, I am mostly able to forget about my pain and focus on the game. Truthfully, there are times when I have to play through some difficult moments—like when I can't see out of one eye or the pain is severe. That's when I remind myself to play through it and be there for my partner.

I've become good at hiding my pain. However, there are days when I just can't get out of bed. I was always a resilient kid. Living with TN and living fully, just proves my resilience.

We left Bend and moved to Florida in 2021 to make a change. The housing market in Bend was skyrocketing and it was a good time to cash out. I wanted to be closer to flights to London so I could visit my parents more often. I have a brother who has only seen me play on TV. My parents are huge fans. They are fully invested and support everything I do. So we moved to the Villages in Florida. It was still during the pandemic, so things were shut down and there wasn't much we could do. I stopped playing tennis and made a full switch to pickleball.

There weren't many tournaments in 2021. I spent my time concentrating on competing, improving, playing more intentionally, teaching and being active in the camp and clinic world. That was when I was recruited to play on the MLP team (Major League Pickleball). My team did very well and so did I personally. I was crowned the MVP of the inaugural MLP event. This was a tremendous achievement for me and launched me in my breakout year. That's when I started playing more and teaching less. Soon after I became a strategic advisor for DUPR, dealing with leagues and international partnerships and helping grow the game. As a sponsored player, I continue to play MLP and play on the APP Tour.

The ball doesn't care that I have come to this sport older than my fellow pro tour players. I imagine in another five years I wouldn't have had the same opportunities I've had at my age, as the sport is rapidly evolving to a younger group of players.

I am very grateful to be able to play as a pro, be relevant and work in the field of pickleball. It has brought so much joy and enhanced so many people's lives. I always said tennis would always be a part of my life, I lied. But now I say with conviction: pickleball will always be a part of my life. This time I mean it.

The most inspiring thing for me is that I have a front row seat to the growth of this game. I get to transform people's lives daily. I love all the amateurs' stories: those dealing with chemo, the loss of a child, a wounded warrior–everyone has their own internal battle and struggle. We are all a coalition of misfits out there. Pickleball is an extension of the community. It is the conduit for socializing. It's everyone's backyard.

There are essentially three spaces for adults: work, home and maybe church. Many have found pickleball to be one of the best adult spaces for connection. It doesn't take a lot of skill to play, there is very little barrier to entry and it is mostly very welcoming.

Pickleball is a lifeline for me. I am so lucky to be in this space. I feel it's very important that the fans are a part of my journey. I like to acknowledge them. My wins and losses aren't as important as those relationships. I engage with them on Instagram and Facebook. It's a thank you. I see you. I'm out here because you give me this platform. In turn I encourage you to embrace the fun. Keep everything in perspective and celebrate together.

Tracy Wilcox

On the Pickleball Highwire

Pickleball is a balancing act for me. I am becoming who I will be, while being who I am. The act requires me to walk a line of humility versus confidence, graciousness versus competitiveness and patience in the process versus anxiousness to become better. It also fosters an eagerness to keep becoming better versus contentment with what I have already achieved. The process has been a paradox of humility yet bolsters my confidence, unsteady yet steadying, and lonely yet filled with community.

My childhood happened on the soccer and basketball field. My family unit consisted of my mom, dad and my sister, thirteen months older than me. Our difference in age created a prickly atmosphere of competitiveness in our household. Kim was a star athlete and brilliant student. I was a hard-working athlete and an adequate student. I lived in her shadow and it felt rotten. Meanwhile, my family spent every weekend either at the basketball court or soccer field. During the week, we attended practices and when there was no practice, we were out shooting basketballs at the hoop behind our house. I adored playing basketball, but more importantly I loved the grind of practices and playing games.

When it was time for me to start high school, I did not want to attend the school where my dad was the principal and my sister was the star athlete and academic genius. I needed to find my own space and become my own person. The irony was that this change put me in direct competition with my sister–since our school soccer and basketball teams played against each other. When the announcer called out the starting lineup for our high school basketball games, we would meet in the middle and hug. Those moments are forever etched in our treasured family photos.

Living in the shadow of my father and sister was the hardest part of my childhood. The inadequacy would haunt me into adulthood. Admittedly, I carried a chip on my shoulder that still prompts me to be out in front. Sometimes it leads me to be defensive at any suggestion that I am less than I am. It has been both the fire that fuels me to achieve, while at the same time the emotional barrier that can block me from moving forward. Believing in myself continues to be one of my greatest obstacles.

After high school, I attended the University of Northern Colorado, where I finished a degree in education, met my husband Dave, and shortly after started our family. I turned my love for basketball and soccer into youth coaching, being one of the very few female coaches in most of the leagues where I coached. By 2004, we had three children and started the process of adopting children from China and Ethiopia. By 2014, our family would grow to seven: four biological and three adopted children.

In April of 2012, as we prepared to depart for Ethiopia to bring home our two children, Dave and I discovered the US Embassy would deny our son his visa into the United States. We made the tough decision for me to leave my four young children and husband in Santa Barbara while I waited in Ethiopia with our newly adopted children until we were able to return. For two months, I lived in a third-world country with two emotionally needy children with whom I did not share a language. We hired a lawyer, a private investigator and fought many battles to finally enable us to come home in June of 2012. This experience continues to be the hardest thing I have ever done. On the positive side, it also gave me confidence to know I can do hard things and not only survive but thrive. We completed our family in 2014 with the arrival of our daughter from China.

Following the adoptions, I spent years in the muck helping my children heal from the trauma of adoption, teaching them English, learning how to care for natural black hair, and acclimating to being a large, multi-racial family. During this time, I was still committed to youth sports by continuing to coach all my children in their various sports at the recreational and club levels.

In 2018, our friend Kara Williams introduced Dave and me to pickleball. We were instantly fans of the sport. As my friend Kara now relates, I was "horrible at the sport--athletic but really couldn't hit a ball." My friend Holly and I learned about open play at our local courts, so we made a date and decided to give it a try. It was like junior high school all over again. We had to decide what court to put our paddles on and then hope they did not reject us. With sweaty palms and a nervous stomach we apprehensively joined in. It took a lot of courage that first time on the court. I'm thankful for the kind people who helped me to learn the game and encouraged me those first days.

Being an ultra-competitive person and seeing that I was not the best player on the courts, drove me to dig in and look for ways to become better. I was frustrated by my lack of skill. I was happy to learn that the local senior pro, Dayne Gingrich, gave lessons and ran clinics. I was all in. Dayne's innate ability to coach individuals in both the mental and physical part of the game was what I needed to help propel me to advance my level. During our first conversation, Dayne challenged Dave and me "to become the best in Santa Barbara." This has been my goal ever since.

As I work toward that goal, opportunities have unfolded along the way. The local public court teaching pro, who was giving clinics and lessons, was moving out of town. That opening allowed Dave and me to assume her position. Over the course of a year we became certified to teach pickleball and are now the local coaching pros in Santa Barbara.

All things pickleball consume a good portion of my day, between playing, drilling, and teaching. I witness firsthand how the sport has transformed people's lives and the recreational subculture in our community. My proudest moments are stepping onto the courts and seeing students from our clinics playing together. Pickleball not only creates a strong community, but also creates a sense of belonging. From recently widowed women and men who need an activity to fill the empty hole, to others who have just recovered from cancer and need a new activity to heal their bodies, pickleball can be transforming.

The sport levels me mentally, emotionally, and physically. I am learning to take the panic out of my game by realizing that the panic comes from my feet. It comes in the intense moments in a game reaching for a difficult ball or in a fast-hand battle at the net. Calming myself by learning to breathe in those intense moments on the court has transferred over to sustaining me in tough moments in my daily life.

The goal of becoming the best in Santa Barbara has greatly informed my daily habits. I practice yoga every day to build muscle and flexibility, ride my bike to improve my cardio and recover, and adjust my diet to eat nutrient dense foods. I schedule in time to drill, watch videos, and focus on neuro-cognitive brain training. I have learned the power of habits. I credit my life in pickleball for being a healthier person: physically, emotionally and mentally.

Tournament play helps me to accept in advance all that I cannot control and what I can control. I have little power over so much, however, learning to take full responsibility for what I can control has helped me to be fully accountable to myself. I am constantly evaluating my actions: how I handle tough opponents, how I support my partner and how I mentally endure the process. Evaluating my progress yields important information for me. It's humbling to realize that sometimes I am not the best partner and that I can mentally let down during a game. However, this process refines me. If I can see myself as not only a work in progress but simultaneously as a badass, then I can accept the hard parts of the evolution of my progress.

Playing pickleball is a critical apparatus in helping me heal from past wounds and removing that inadequate self chip off my shoulder. The sport has helped me learn to balance emotionally, spiritually, mentally and physically. Emotionally, I am now able to develop a belief in myself at the deepest level that allows self-confirmation to know that I am loved and valuable. Spiritually, my faith and understanding of my worth in God's eyes is a foundational tenet of who I am. Mentally, playing pickleball stretches me to endure pain and agitation and is foundational in making me a stronger and more poised person. Physically, pickleball can push me, break me down, and build me back up. Combining all my past experiences as a coach, as an athlete, and now as a wife and mother, I believe I am in exactly the right place at this moment, with pickleball as an equalizing driving force.

In February of 2022, our life would take another turn and head us in our current direction–fulfilling our dreams. It is quite ironic that it would take a medical emergency to get us there. Dave and I were over-stretched with different businesses and community commitments and we were feeling overwhelmed. This stress caused a cluster of blood vessels in my husband's brain to leak and resulted in the seizures. After a night in the emergency and many visits to doctors, we are very thankful for a positive outcome and medication that helps him control his seizures.

It was a wake-up call for us. We revamped our lives to align with our dreams. We were spending our energy on projects that were no longer part of our long-term vision. We maneuvered our time and money to realign. That realignment would put us on the road to selling a house in Santa Barbara and purchasing a dying tennis club in Harker Heights, Texas. We bought it, rebranded it as Heights Athletic Club, built five beautiful covered pickleball courts, four permanent courts and restored the heartbeat of an underused club. In the same month we started the Santa Barbara Pickleball Club in Santa Barbara, California.

Our dream is simple. We want to roll out of bed, put on our pickleball shoes, go to the courts, teach and play pickleball, and go home take off our pickleball shoes and be with our family. Ironically we removed the stress and then added more stress. Currently, we are spending every waking minute building our new businesses. This stress is worth it, as we know our energy is now being used in the direction we want to go and we see the destination clearly on the horizon.

Nancy Yocono

Pickleball: Give it a Try

I was attending a hula hoop class offered at a local school gym seven years ago. Following my class, there was a beginner pickleball lesson taking place. An energetic, enthusiastic woman was inviting all in her view to give it a try. Since I was always an athletic person and open to trying new things, I decided to give it a try. She offered compassionate training and paddles to use.

There were people of all ages and abilities, which made the class inviting. Surprisingly, I was hooked from the beginning. My goal was to get my own paddle. It was not easy to find one. I ordered online, having no idea what I was getting. My first paddle was a Wilson, that I knew was a good brand in tennis. The weight and response were so much better than the wooden one I had been using. I quickly noticed the ease of playing with a better paddle. As a benefit, I no longer experienced the arm pain that I had been dealing with for a while.

The beginner indoor winter class extended to outdoors in the late spring, summer and fall. The opportunity for enjoyable exercise and to meet other active people meshed well with my desire to socialize and experience overall well-being. As word spread about the game, it provided additional venues and a larger pickleball community. More and more schools and rec programs started to offer playtime. Many of us did not know what it was back then, pickleball? Whenever I would mention it a description was also in order. Initially it was described as an old person's tennis. This is no longer an accurate description. It was also described as a cross between badminton and ping pong.

I am tall and a bigger person. My height seems to frustrate lobbers and my overall size often has others underestimate my agility and ability. In addition, I am also a senior woman who often plays with younger people. I enjoy the look of surprise I get from them too. There are definitely days I can't seem to play at all and other days I feel like a pro. I enjoy playing with people of all ages and abilities as long as we keep it fun. I often have to remind myself of this when I start to get too serious or frustrated. Even though I was able to get into this sport with very little investment, its popularity has certainly driven up prices. I'm glad that it's still possible to get started without a big financial commitment. Indoor venues often have a day fee or membership and when the weather requires it I pay. However, most of the time it is free play outdoors.

I will often spend time with an underdog to help build their confidence. Although I am very competitive and like to win, I do not enjoy playing with those that must win all the time. I am finding so much joy and delight in not taking this game too seriously. I have thought about competing to be able to get an accurate ranking and say that I did it. However I've heard some say the fun of the game does not exist in competition. Maybe I need to find that out. Depending on the group playing, sometimes I find being a woman can become an issue. There are some guys that just want to play with guys. Fortunately, most of my encounters are open to all.

Just recently a female friend and I were approaching full courts and she backed away saying it was all men so she would not be playing. I hadn't noticed as I'm often the only woman.

I have fallen, been injured and thankfully have been able to heal and get back in the game. I have overplayed, pushing morning and night every day. When I do this my body pays the price. Icing and ibuprofen are my go-to rescues. I'd like to think I have now learned that just because I want to play and can play, doesn't mean I should play. Rest and body recoup is very important, as are warm-ups and cool-downs, particularly as we age.

Pickleball for me is a healthy addictive activity. The laughter, usually at myself, the friendships, the opportunities for improvement and the vast amount of places to play now is marvelous. I am proud that I am now that energetic enthusiastic person inviting everyone I see to give it a try. I carry around extra paddles just in case someone new shows up.

Co-Author Dotti Berry

Coach B was born to coach. She's been doing that for 55 years. From coaching women's basketball at the University of Kentucky to facilitating groups at Esprit Transgender Conference, her work as a coach continues to be diverse. Her business was Lexington, KY Chamber of Commerce Small Business of the Year and also ASI (Advertising Specialty Institute) Small Business of the Year in the U.S. She resides in Blaine, WA, with her wife, Robynne Sapp, Baylee Joy and Willow Joy. As the Pickleball MindShift Coach, she works with women both on and off the court. She is an Ambassador with USAPA and certified as a coach with PPR, IPTPA and Helle Sparre's Dynamite Doubles. Dotti loves working in the field of recovery and staying healthy with everyday people and pros who play pickleball utilizing BEMER https://coachb.bemergroup.com Dotti's best skill is her ability to connect people with one another and then engage them through her visionary way of celebrating women in pickleball. A paddle in one hand of a commissioned sculpture by Thomas Vrba birthed EmPOWER, coinciding with Dotti's vision to collect the empowering stories of both everyday rec and tournament players, as well as professionals. She created Pickleball Unites with a global vision of transcending differences that separate us, collaborating to bring together people and resources for life-changing experiences, one country at a time. You can reach Dotti at 888-440-9780 and through the various pickleball entities she has created.

Pickleball Unites: www.PickleballUnites.com
Pickleball Forum For Women Facebook group:
https://bit.ly/PickleballForumForWomen
Pickleball Happy Hour: https://bit.ly/PickleballHappyHour
Pickleball Events for Women: https://bit.ly/PFFWevents
Pickleball MindShift Coaching: https://bit.ly/PickleballMindShiftWebinars
Rosie "We Can Do It" Paddle: https://bit.ly/PFFW-RosiePaddle

Co-Author Jody Belsher

A native of Skokie, Illinois, Jody made her way to California as a singer/songwriter. While in Santa Monica, she was cycling, running and playing tennis and eventually competed in a number of triathlons and half-marathons. She owned an entertainment PR and personal management firm prior to moving to the Central Coast of California with her husband John and three children. She is currently training for the Camino de Santiago 500 mile walk across Spain, known as "The Way." Jody attended UCLA Public Relations courses and was a student in the master's program at the USC School of Journalism. She also earned a Master's in Addictive Disorders from the Breining Institute. As a Support Coach, Jody has assisted numerous individuals and families struggling with addiction issues. She has produced three documentaries. One of her films took first place in a Los Angeles film festival and is shown worldwide. Her interests include calligraphy, quilting and songwriting—she plays guitar and piano. Trained as a graphic artist, Jody continues to create artwork and is the creator of the Pickleball Workbook©, a journal/planner for the advancing player. She is the CEO of a promising start-up software company, along with her partner Oumar Sall from Paris, France. Jody partnered with Dotti Berry on the creation of the EmPOWER book and through interviewing many of the authors has had an enlightening experience. Jody is a Nana to six grandchildren and has a big heart for animals—including her two dogs and a cat. Jody played two years on the Cuesta College tennis team at 39-40 years old and was nominated Athlete of the Year. She is an avid golfer, hiker and swimmer and played many years of sand volleyball. After coaching high school teams as a USTA certified coach and competing in numerous tennis matches, Jody was introduced to pickleball. She is enjoying competing in pickleball tournaments across the U.S. where she has connected with many wonderful people along the way. Jody can be reached at:

jbcreative1@gmail.com, www.jbelsher.com, www.pickleballworkbook.com

Thank you for reading these powerful stories and supporting our labor of love. Pickleball may be just a sport for some, but for many it has been a life-changing experience. We appreciate your interest and wish you the best with all your endeavors.

EmPOWER is available on Amazon and can be located on our website: www.empowerpickleballwomen.com

Please share with your friends and family.

Made in the USA
Las Vegas, NV
03 August 2023

75585748R00144